10 *Contemporary*
Polish Stories

10 Contemporary Polish Stories

translated by various hands

and edited by Edmund Ordon

with an introduction by

Olga Scherer-Virski

Detroit   Wayne State University Press   1958

Library of Congress
Catalog Card Number 58-6988

Copyright 1958
Wayne State University Press
Detroit 2, Michigan

Preface

*J*n a few years Poland will celebrate its thousandth
year as a nation. It is fitting to recognize and to com-
memorate an event of such magnitude before and after it
occurs. This selection of Polish short stories is the first
of a series of publications intended to make available to
the American reader some of the fruits of Poland's long
history. Succeeding volumes will present other aspects
and periods of Polish cultural achievements.

The brief notes which precede the stories are not meant
to be exhaustive. They are intended simply to provide
some information about the authors and, where necessary,
to help explain matters which an American reader may
find unfamiliar. Personal names and place names have, in
general, been retained in their Polish forms.

The preparation of this book was greatly lightened by
the willing and generous cooperation of all concerned. To

the authors still living who appear in it I am indebted for their generous permission to use their stories. Polish authorities promptly granted my request to publish stories by the two authors who are no longer living. To my widely-scattered co-translators I am grateful for their ready and undemanding assistance. I wish to express particular gratitude to Olga Scherer-Virski, Aleksander Janta and Wiktor Weintraub for their helpful concern with the whole of this book.

Edmund Ordon
Wayne State University

Contents

vii

CONTENTS

Acknowledgments

Acknowledgment is made to the following for permission
to use the short story selections, and translations, included
in this volume:

To Maria Dąbrowska for "Father Philip."

To Kazimierz Wierzyński for "Patrol" and Julius Balbin
for his translation.

To Michał Choromański for "A Cynical Tale" and Thad
Kowalski for his translation.

To Jerzy Ros, Press and Cultural Attaché of the Em-
bassy of the Polish People's Republic, for Bruno Schulz's
"My Father Joins the Fire Brigade" and Piotr Choynowski's "Boarding House" and W. Stanley Moss and
Zofia Tarnowska, and Helen Jankowska for their respec-
tive translations.

ACKNOWLEDGMENTS

To Maria Kuncewiczowa for "A Turban" and George J. Maciuszko for his translation.

To Witold Gombrowicz for "Premeditated Crime" and Olga Scherer-Virski for her translation.

To Józef Mackiewicz for "The Adventures of an Imp" and Bronislas de Leval Jezierski for his translation.

To Jerzy Zawieyski for "The President Calls" and Adam Czerniawski for his translation.

To Marek Hłasko for "The Most Sacred Words of Our Life" and Wojciech Gniatczyński and Adam Czerniawski for their translation.

Introduction

OLGA SCHERER-VIRSKI

$\mathcal{T}$he purpose of this publication is to offer to the American reader several samples of short stories written by Polish authors in the last three decades. Without attempting to produce an anthology in the strict sense of the word, which would have entailed a larger number of stories chosen from the works of representative writers only, the editor and his assistants have tried to compile a selection of short stories by authors who are well known to the Polish reading public, works varying in quality, originality and importance.

The first principle which guided the selection was the translatability, linguistic as well as cultural, from the original Polish. Several fine specimens of the short prose genre were eliminated upon consideration of the loss translation into a foreign language and cultural climate would inflict on otherwise irreproachable pieces of literature. The second criterion was that the volume should contain products of only those authors whose writings, or at least short stories, had never before been published in an English translation, or had been published only in little known and difficult to obtain periodicals.

An effort was made to keep in mind the strict definition of the nature and function of the short story as a separate, autonomous genre in world literature. Independent from the novel, and in a structural sense perhaps even in opposition to it, a short story is a work of fiction which lives by virtue of the singleness of the effect it produces. It requires a maximal economy of means with a maximal utilization of its devices for the purpose of the realization of a unified, frequently dramatic, effect. Even though some of the pieces included in this book form part of larger works, or cycles, they unquestionably fulfill the strict tasks which literary tradition has assigned to the short story.

Modern Polish prose fiction evolved throughout the nineteenth century in the shadow of Western Europe. Romanticism, with its poetic, sometimes supernatural, tale, gave way to realism in the latter part of the century. It was then that the Polish short story was crystallized into a unique genre and perfected in the artistic quality of its devices with such writers as Bolesław Prus, Maria Konopnicka, Henryk Sienkiewicz and particularly Zygmunt Niedźwiecki, the "Polish Maupassant." The influence of a purely Polish source of the modern short story, the early nineteenth-century *gawęda*, an informal yarn-spinning tale, casual in style and loose in structure, having survived the intransigent conception of the short story during the epoch of realism and the turn-of-the-

century modernism (Stefan Żeromski, Władysław Rey-
mont), can still occasionally be detected in the informal
tone sometimes assumed by certain more recent and even
contemporary writers.

Ten twentieth-century short stories have been set as the
goal of this first volume of a series of English translations
from Polish literature. It is with considerable regret that
we leave unrepresented the works of a great many stimu-
lating writers. We must even omit mentioning them here,
for their names alone would have no meaning to the
English reader.

The first seven stories included in the volume were
produced in the 1920's or 1930's in the normal literary conditions of a free country by authors most of whom are
still alive and active. The period between the two World
Wars was so varied, so far as short story writing in Poland
is concerned, that it is impossible to suggest any of its
dominant traits as characteristic. Suffice it to say that it
is variety that constitutes its most distinguishing feature.

The natural development of Polish literature was interrupted by the War of 1939–1945 and by the subsequent
involuntary submission of the country and its entire cultural life to the Soviet conqueror. Reverting to a familiar
historical precedent, the Polish writers split into two
groups, the one at home, the other in exile, as they had
done after the failure of the Polish insurrection against
Russia in 1831.

The financially unendowed but politically free writers
in exile have centered their literary activities chiefly
around the two best periodical publications in exile: the
weekly *Wiadomości (News)* in London, and the monthly
Kultura (Culture) in Paris. In recent years several books

xiii

of Polish short stories have appeared in France and in England. In addition to the story by Józef Mackiewicz, we should have liked to include several other examples of stories written abroad, especially those produced by writers of the younger generation, whose literary debut took place in exile. The one incontestable statement that may by now be made about the Polish short story abroad, as indeed it may also be made about other genres, especially poetry, is that its function of providing prewar and wartime reminiscences is gradually giving way to more immediate preoccupations. The émigré writers thus greatly enrich the Polish story by injecting into it new, occasionally exotic elements of the customs and values of the various countries they inhabit.

After an initial period of relative freedom immediately following the war, the stifling canons of the Soviet-enforced so-called "social realism," the inflexible practices of censorship and the isolation from earlier Polish traditions and from contemporary Western literary trends paralyzed the creative talents in Poland. This is not the proper place in which to pass judgment on those authors whose fear of the Communist Party was stronger than their loyalty to art throughout the grimmest years of oppression. We may say, and time will further show, that their number does not surpass that of the fighters for freedom who were either silenced or who filled their drawers with works unacceptable to the regime.

Before we turn to the presentation of the individual authors singled out for this book, let us say that the timid revival of real literature in Poland, after approximately fifteen years of virtual silence, gave us at least part of the impulse needed to undertake this translation project.

II

To present the short stories of Maria Dąbrowska, the matriarch of Polish contemporary letters and the first author figuring in this volume, without a few remarks about the general manner of her writing, the discretion and measured pace of her artistry, which have already in the writer's lifetime raised her works to the level of classics in Polish literature, is a precarious task. Author of one of the longest novels ever written in Polish, Dąbrowska is also a skillful and prolific writer of short stories. Her high class of realism, which shies away from emphasizing "types," and heightens individual characteristics and concentrates on that which is both vulnerable and disarming in human nature, is clearly visible in *People From Over There,* an early collection of stories, published in the 1920's, in which a peasant community comes to life in the course of several sensitive character sketches.

"Father Philip" forms part of Dąbrowska's second well known book of short stories, *Signs of Life.* Its reserved, patient tone, the length of the introductory part, which precedes the actual opening of the action, is indicative of a conservative type of short story which may strike the reader as old-fashioned. Dąbrowska's intention is neither to startle nor to shock the reader.

Though she preserves the essentially pessimistic undertone of every writer of quality, hers is a pessimism devoid of malice or despair; her characters, who are neither saints nor villains, move in a world at whose injustices she glances with tolerant resignation rather than with bitterness or invectives. The richness of minute detail compensates for the lack of any tense external action in her stories; and the simple lyricism of her style, the compactness of accurate, ironical aphorisms which adorn the narration, have remained salient features of her work throughout her long and varied career.

After a long winter of literature filled with paperdoll characters involved in false problems, puppets given to artificial social optimism and political enthusiasm, fulfilling inhuman economic tasks with the same unauthentic alacrity which had moved their authors to fulfill the task of creating them, it is not by accident that one of the first daring signs of the literary "thaw," which began in Poland in 1954, should have emerged under the pen of Maria Dąbrowska. It is the short story "A Wedding in the Country," which shyly but firmly returns real people to the world of literature.

III

One of the finest literary documents in prose to have come out of the first World War is Kazimierz Wierzyński's volume of short stories *The Frontiers of the World*, from which our second selection, "Patrol," has been taken. It would be difficult to divine from its factual, apparently insensitive, sometimes even terse, prose the hand of one of Poland's most excellent lyric poets between the two World Wars and, without a doubt, the greatest and most prolific poet in exile today.

A youthful officer in the Austrian Army, fighting on the Russian front, Wierzyński describes with authority the grim front-line setting and the detrimental effect of the absurdity of warfare on individual behavior. Although World War I is treated calmly, as a natural manifestation

of inevitable forces, its historical paradox emerges, unde-
liberately perhaps, as that of the war which put an end
to nineteenth-century morality, thus releasing contemporary chaos. Wierzyński's calm, his conscious under-
statement, together with the naturalistic descriptions of
such horrors of war as hunger, disease, the shocking appearance of decaying bodies, his sparingly used humor
and irony, enhanced by a strictly enforced economy of
means in the structure of the stories, lay open the pathos
of the world catastrophe.

The cruel irony of military operations achieves the
utmost simplicity of expression in "Patrol," the inconspicuous central figure of which, a peasant "ridiculously small
against the bare measureless space," becomes the symbol
of the peaceful world of simple people, caught in the midst
of an irrational conflict they neither want nor understand,
a conflict which plays far beyond the level of their own
conception of life.

IV

Our third selection, "A Cynical Tale," constitutes, together with three other stories, entitled respectively
"Banal," "Incredible" and "Insane," Michał Choromański's
volume of short stories of the 1930's, *Ambiguous Tales*.
The enormous success in Europe of Choromański's strik-
ingly original novel *Jealousy and Medicine* has eclipsed
his interesting tales even among Polish readers.

Choromański's imaginary elements are deliberately
commonplace, the events around which the stories are
woven, trivial, and the stories themselves, consciously
blown up and extended. Attention is focused on details,

especially on the details of action, with several potential meanings attributed to them. The skillful anticipation of events accentuates the triviality of the drama by seemingly taking the edge off it. In this respect "A Cynical Tale" is even more banal than the "Banal Tale" itself. The variety of temporal perspectives is matched by the cinematographic device of differentiated psychological perspectives, permitting the "event" to emerge as an anti-climax.

Unlike "A Cynical Tale," where the thin action is sustained by a mysterious, elaborately built up suspense, "An Incredible Tale" has the appearances of a plot stripped of all its enigma, down to the bare outline of its structure. It consists of a series of cables and letters, containing pleas for financial help, sent to relatives and friends by a man who gambled himself into precarious debt at Monte Carlo, and of accompanying flashbacks which describe the former relations between the hero and the recipients of his desperate messages. Although the motifs change from story to story, the style throughout the volume is preserved at the level of factual reporting, verging on dryness, and the atmosphere keeps a uniformly morbid character.

The film industry of America and Europe has regrettably overlooked the excellence of Choromański's works, particularly his short novel *The White Brothers,* as potential scenarios for artistically superior, sophisticated thrillers.

V

The Cinnamon Shops, Bruno Schulz's masterpiece of 1936, a frightening fantasy made up of loosely connected fragments and tales, could have been created by Franz Kafka. Its central character, the narrator's father, assailed by the irrationality of the surrounding reality, becomes the victim of hallucinations; he fades away, literally becoming smaller in size. This folly is then followed by another, namely that of behaving (and appearing) like a bird, hatching the eggs of expensive exotic species, flying about in his room, often perched on a curtain-rod, until he gradually turns into a cockroach and disappears together with the sweepings.

By a curious artistic feat Schulz achieves more dramatic suspense in those stories which are completely devoid of action. In "Pan" he goes on for pages unwinding the drama of the static elements of nature and urban filth in order to introduce at the end only one human being, if human he be, a terrible vagabond, the surrealistic apparition of the mythological Pan. "Karol," another story in which again "nothing happens," presents, as it were, the non-realistic counterpart of the Russian hero of passivity, Oblomov, the narrator's Uncle Karol, a superfluous man, as he rises from bed in the morning. "And so, half tossed out of the depth of sleep, he hung for a while, unconscious, on the edge of the night, catching air into his lungs, while all round him the bed linen swelled and fermented and covered him again with its folds of heavy, whitish dough." [1] The comparison between the bed sheets and dough, it should be said in passing, runs through the entire story, just as the father's fear of, and fascination for, cockroaches runs through the entire text.

[1] Bruno Schulz, *Sklepy cynamonowe* [*The Cinnamon Shops*], (Warsaw, 1934), p. 122.

A consistent feature in *The Cinnamon Shops* is Schulz's attribution of active human traits to inanimate objects. The book abounds in such statements as "white days, astonished and unnecessary"; "furniture which tolerated him in silence." Another trait all the stories have in common is their wealth of digressions.

The Schulz fantasy, no doubt, deserves a complete translation into English. Meanwhile, we offer "My Father Joins the Fire Brigade," one of his later stories from the collection entitled *Sanatorium Under the Hourglass* which resembles *The Cinnamon Shops* in that its action also deals with the same four central figures, the father, the mother, the servant girl Adela and the adolescent narrator Joseph. Less accomplished as works of art, these tales can, nevertheless, be more readily presented out of the context of the larger unit to which they belong.

VI

The simple anecdote, "Boarding House," introduces us into a very different atmosphere of adolescent life. Its author Piotr Choynowski, who wrote a great deal about the events preceding the first World War, felt particularly at home in handling agitated action. Frequently associated with a sympathetic satire against the foibles of adolescence, he was eminently able to glorify the nobility of its feelings. A valid instance of the latter may be found in the story entitled "A Deed," in which a poor love-stricken schoolboy perishes in a street fight in 1905 in order to save the life of his richer and more successful rival. The hero's self-analysis, entirely free from sentimentality and yet unveiled with the most intense lyricism, is of the highest literary quality.

Lighthearted satire is also a salient trait of Choynowski's numerous character sketches, a number of which fall into an unusual type of the short genre of fiction, the historical short story. Although this type of short story had been cultivated on a modest scale by European authors of the nineteenth century, notably by Balzac, Polish fiction, though rich in historical novels, particularly historical war novels, contains only rare specimens of the historical tale. This is particularly true in the twentieth century. The Polish reader is accustomed chiefly to the short story in a contemporaneous setting. Choynowski's tales of the early eighteenth century remind us of the nineteenth-century casual tale, the *gawęda*, not only because of the remote epoch they treat, but especially because of their informal tone, the authenticity of style and the evocation of an old-fashioned graciousness. Conscious of the temporal distance between himself and his subject, ideologically uncommitted with regard to a dead, completely harmless world, Choynowski attenuates the *gawęda* type of brashness with subtle notes of uncritical irony, sparing the reader both condemnation and nostalgia.

VII

Author of several novels, among them *The Stranger*, which was translated into nine languages before the second World War, Maria Kuncewiczowa (Kuncewicz) is also a talented short story writer.

Like Dąbrowska's pieces in *People From Over There*,

all the stories in Kuncewiczowa's *Two Moons,* her best know collection, share the unity of time and place, since the protagonist of one short story sinks into the background of others. The title story cleverly introduces all the major characters of the two worlds: the local population of a small picturesque town on the banks of the Vistula and a group of Warsaw artists who spend the summer of 1930 there. The moon, the duality of which stresses the difference between these two worlds, appears in nearly all these brief, highly concentrated pieces as one of the economical, almost stingy elements of the description of nature.

Kuncewiczowa's bold, general strokes, which admirably evoke an atmosphere in its totality, and a style which varies from story to story, depending on the point of view of the main character, help her achieve the rare success of writing interestingly about artists, without risking the dangerous penetration of a painter's creative process. The factual delineation of the plot rests upon the cornerstones of a few, emphatically signaled *realia.* The realism, deeper than that exhibited by faithful, detailed description, concerns traditional characters familiar on the Polish prewar scene. The originality of these tales lies in the imponderable complexes, weaknesses or yearnings, they portray in the heroes, against the stylized background of a traditionally defined behavior. In some of the stories the two mutually unintelligible worlds clash in an outburst of dramatic action, as in "Strange Rachel," where a city painter immortalizes on canvas the artistically appealing sight of a small Jewish girl playing with the reflection of the sun in a dirty stream, an occupation which is shocking both to the girl's simple-minded parents and their ally, the painter's impoverished but well-educated aunt. Something similar occurs in "The Island," in which a local policeman is incapable of grasping the strange practices of the sophisticated group of artists. In "A Turban," the sixth story included in this selection, the action flows within the extravagant artists' colony, but the reality of the world from under "the other moon," the world of peasants, fruitgrowers, shopkeepers, Jewish merchants and artisans, is delicately juxtaposed in the form of the poor Jewish luggage porter who is contrasted with the hero Simon.

In a new émigré edition of *Two Moons*, the author writes in the introduction: "And so—good or bad—the book about the moons over the Vistula has probably not ceased to be up to date. Some of its characters have bodily disappeared from the scene of Polish life, but they have remained there in spirit."[2]

VIII

As we undertake now the presentation of the most original prose writer of the 1930's, Witold Gombrowicz, whose creative energies have only increased in his distant exile in Argentina, we must warn the reader that the author's manner, though splendidly unique and recognizable throughout his career, has greatly evolved and perfected itself since the publication in 1936 of his first work, the collection of tales under the common title *The Diary of a*

[2] Maria Kuncewiczowa, *Dwa Księżyce [Two Moons]*, (London, 1954), p. 10.

Young Man, from which we selected "Premeditated Crime" for this volume.

In his own recent reminiscences Gombrowicz writes that the celebrated novel *Ferdydurke,* his second work written in 1936–1937, is "existential to the bone." [3] We shall leave it to the reader to conclude whether the same statement would apply to the youthful *Diary of a Young Man,* or at least to our selection from it, but let us call attention to the fact that the characters in "Premeditated Crime" are mutually created and built into the form which defines them—clearly a condition of existence rather than of essence. The narrator is pulled into the game of a "pre-arranged theatrical scene" which dictates the rules for all his moves. The four characters are interlocked within a mysterious distribution of elements which, no matter how false in their objective appearances, nevertheless possess a certain deeper, philosophic veracity. This underlying truthfulness of a seeming incompatibility comes out even more forcefully in "A Supper Party at the Countess Kotłubaj's" (in my opinion the best but regrettably the least translatable story of the group), where a peasant boy named Cauliflower freezes to death in front of the Countess' palace; though not actually identified with the vegetable by that name, which is being simultaneously eaten at the table of the grotesque countess and her decadent friends, the boy becomes, through a deft parallel, the victim of inherent cannibalistic instincts.

Supernatural dreams and fantastic associations in such stories as "Adventures on the Banbury" or "Five Minutes Before Sleep" aid in unveiling one of Gombrowicz's chief

[3] Witold Gombrowicz, "Fragmenty z Dziennika" ["Fragments from a Journal"], *Kultura,* Paris (April, 1956), 44.

preoccupations, the basic changes which operate in a person's emotions and behavior when he is transferred into new and different surroundings. The arbitrariness of the linguistic sign indirectly becomes an object of attack in Gombrowicz's works.

Several of his products, including the difficult play *The Marriage*, have the makings of brilliant screenplays. In this, but only in this one respect, may they be said to resemble some of Michał Choromański's agitated pieces of fiction.

IX

Józef Mackiewicz (not to be confused with his brother Stanisław Mackiewicz, historian and publicist, who recently chose to return to Poland from political exile in London) is a most gifted and prolific writer. In addition to infrequent short stories, more frequent humorous pieces, Józef Mackiewicz has produced a number of full-length books. Of these his novel *A Road to Nowhere* is probably the most significant in its unsentimental interpretation of one of the aspects of the contemporary epic of Polish suffering and pilgrimage, dealing with the Soviet occupation of Polish Lithuania in 1940 and the ensuing loss of political freedom, arrests, deportations and attempts at escape. He possesses the memory of a journalist, the style of a man of letters, the objectivity of a scientist and the caution of a critic. Speaking of criticism, we must include Józef Mackiewicz amongst the most astute Polish social (and literary) critics in exile. Independent, sometimes even lonely, in his judgment, he has contributed not only interesting essays on literature, Polish and foreign (he is a great admirer of nineteenth-century Russian literature), but also critical pieces about the international situation and recent history, often elucidating its obscure or inconspicuous aspects, articles on émigré life, politics, writers and publications. He pitilessly criticizes various signs of complacency in intellectual émigré circles.

"Adventures of an Imp" is an example of an allegorical tale written by an accomplished journalist and critic. This fable, which adds questions of international politics and world diplomacy to problems of good and evil as manifested in the private lives of individuals, pokes fun at the primitive tenets of our morality, the monolithic manner of reasoning, and the lack of nuances in the ideologies of contemporary society.

X

The last two selections in this book, Jerzy Zawieyski's "The President Calls" and Marek Hłasko's "The Most Sacred Words of Our Lives," represent two examples of literature in Poland since the death of Stalin and the subsequent relaxation of the deadly regulations of social realism in literature.

A playwright and novelist reared in the Western literary traditions of prewar Poland, Zawieyski is one of those authors who, along with Maria Dąbrowska and scores of others, has been able to preserve a considerable measure of artistic integrity in spite of the ruthless terror which reigned in Poland between 1948 and 1954. Zawieyski, however, is an ultraconservative writer; the problems he treats in his stories are simple and old-fashioned, involving metaphysically motivated suicides, candid situations of unfulfilled affection and love triangles, most of them occurring among representatives of the former educated middle class, the *intelligentsia* of prewar Poland. Music, which tells the tale of torn emotions and philosophic doubt, in the short story "The Peace of Depth," where the "bourgeois" solution of suicide is introduced, or in *Hubert's Night*, a short novel published immediately after the war, where emotions inspired by music mingle with the personal suffering resulting from the Nazi occupation, is reminiscent of the tousled manner and the Wagnerian preoccupations of many a writer of the turn of the century. Zawieyski's style is one of fifty years ago, cultured, grave and occasionally sentimental. In his *Lyrical Notebook* of 1956, consisting of one and two-page essays, or prose poems, overflowing with descriptions of nature and their subjective, philosophical interpretations, Zawieyski has shown one way of reacting against the oppressive precepts of *socrealizm*—a reversion to a long-forgotten, obsolete style. But he has also shown another in "The President Calls," first published in 1954, where the dreamland of childhood, with its individual grief of an unloved, unwanted child, returns to supplant the noisy, unrealistic crowds of members of the Junior Communist League, adolescent spies for the Party, grade-school children denouncing their parents to the authorities, "class-conscious," happiness-building, proletarian teen-agers. Though the story may appear as lacking in nuance, it is comforting as an example of Zawieyski's production which has succeeded in glorifying the imagination and circumventing the "fulfillment of norms" in the treatment of issues imposed by the new regime.

An entirely different kind of protest against the false-hood of literature in Communist chains comes in the form of sixteen stories written mostly in 1955 by a very young writer, Marek Hłasko. The editors of the Parisian monthly *Preuves* anticipated us by including in their Polish issue of April, 1957, a French translation of the title story and perhaps the best work in Hłasko's *First Step in the Clouds*. Our own selection, "The Most Sacred Words of Our Life," is a characteristic example of the author's kind of writing: a somewhat bawdy style, a structure quite me-chanical in its recurring refrains and an utterly pessimistic general impression.

In Hłasko's strictly urban world the joyous worker of the Communist propaganda posters becomes a helpless, lonely creature, given to excessive drinking, perplexed by the sadness of his life, yearning for love, but often dis-couraged from fulfilling it. "How much longer will lovers not have a place to live," sighs a young worker, who, for purely material reasons, has to give up the woman he loves, "how much longer will people continue to part be-cause of apartment, laundry. . . ? . . . I do not believe in another hell, but even if there should be such a thing, those bottles, those guys standing under the fence, those people queuing up for meat and the girls in hotels, are a worse hell." [4]

Hłasko's criticism of the contemporary reality and, above all, his attack on man's fate in general, under any regime—both conceived in a Western sense of the free expression of a committed author's conscience in a world which is not the best of all possible worlds—come to a high

[4] Marek Hłasko, *Pierwszy krok w chmurach [First Step in the Clouds]*, (Warsaw, 1956), pp. 156-57.

pitch of drama in the physical aspect and the vague conversation of "the two men on the road" (in a story by that title), who, however remotely, resemble Didi and Gogo, protagonists of the most "decadent" of the "rotten West's" decadent plays, *Waiting for Godot.* If we add to this terrifying vision the masterfully ambiguous, infinitely subtle dialogue between a small-town barber and his customer, a Warsaw journalist, in the story "Everything Has Changed," the most poignant work in the volume, or the friendless old man who for years awaits the postman only to receive a chain letter in the end, and if we remember that, unlike his older colleagues, the twenty-six-year-old author had not known Western culture, the traditional patrimony of Poland until recently, we can forgive him the unevenness of his works, the youthful, sometimes artificial, cynicism and the brash obscenities of some stories, and hope with him and other writers of his generation that the political conditions in his country will allow an ever increasing freedom of expression for literary talent.

10 *Contemporary*
Polish Stories

MARIA DĄBROWSKA (1892–   ) is a major figure in contemporary Polish literature. She is known best perhaps as the author of the long novel *Noce i dnie* (*Nights and Days*), published in 1932–34 and reprinted several times. Her best known collections of short stories are *Ludzie stamtąd* (*People From Over There*), published in 1925, and *Znaki życia* (*Signs of Life*), written between 1929 and 1932. In 1956, she published a new collection entitled *Gwiazda zaranna* (*The Morning Star*). She has also written books for children, plays and publicistic works. Her interest in English and American literature led her to translate the *Diary* of Samuel Pepys. Dąbrowska is a strong force in current Polish letters not only because of her artistic excellence, but also by virtue of her own constancy and moral stature.

EDMUND ORDON, the translator, teaches Polish language and literature at Wayne State University. He has published a translation of Kazimierz Wierzyński's *The Forgotten Battlefield* and articles in scholarly journals concerning Polish literature and its relations with American and English literature.

Father Philip

MARIA DĄBROWSKA

*A*nd thus Philip Jaruga became a priest.

At first, before he entered the seminary, he was not sure whether he wanted to become one, but he trusted his parents who maintained that it would be best so. They were owners of a men's tailor shop in a small town and were disposed toward moving out of this position in society if not themselves then at least through their son. However, they thought that there was no better way to do this than through the priesthood.

"No one asks," they explained to their only son, "what station a priest comes from, for he is of a holy station."

And truly. All the people in the suburbs knew well that the bishop of their diocese had tended geese for his poor peasant father, in a nearby village. And who remembers this; and don't the most eminent men kiss his hands; and does he lack bird's milk in his palace? He is looked upon everywhere as though he were a great man's son, and his parents are no longer peasants but the parents of a bishop.

Philip had to admit that that's how it was, and one could not say that he did not have some desire for such a life. He did not dream of a bishopric, of course, but even an ordinary parsonage seemed a very good future to him and to his parents. Prosperity, people's respect, and work that was not too hard, all things for which everyone strives, seemed particularly attainable in this way without any offense to God, in fact, with great spiritual benefit which comes from a priest's pious living and daily communing with God the Highest.

Nevertheless Philip was undecided, for though he had an inclination toward the religious life, he did not feel called to it. He was afraid that he could not awaken in himself that elevation of the spirit which is necessary for carrying out spiritual duties and that he would not endure in the required celibacy, which was said to be demanded by the oath of priesthood.

The old Jarugas had a different notion about this.

"As to that," they said, "there can be no oath. Just as one can't stop eating so one can't jump out of one's skin, whether it be man's or woman's. Since the Lord Jesus clothed you in such a skin, needing such acquaintance, He cannot make a demand without your feeling its effect on yourself. The only demand is that there be no scandal.

"And as for feeling the call," they explained further, "that, too, will come in time. A person must put himself into everything he does, and how is he to know what his calling is until he begins to do something?"

Philip listened and remained inclined to believe everything agreeably, for being an only son he lived with his parents in a closer union of hearts than other boys his age.

But the parents too had some doubts. His mother sometimes regretted that she would not have any grandsons of Philip. And though she comforted herself with the secret

thought that there are priests whose mothers have someone to nurse and hold in their old age, yet she knew that
she must cast this devious thought away as far as she
could and that counting on such joys was forbidden. Still
other ideas presented themselves. Philip was a handsome
boy and it would probably be possible to arrange a good
and rich marriage for him. He was clever in all his studies
and perhaps could reach a high rank in some capacity.
But none of these ideas had as many good sides as the
priesthood. In no other position did the temporal and
eternal benefits, about which the devout mother was much
concerned, combine so strongly and easily. And none kept
the son for the parents as much as the one which limited
his right to have a family. Thus when the appropriate
time arrived, the occasionally occurring uncertainties
paled and Philip set out for the seminary.

After his departure, his parents at first did not know
what to do with themselves in their sadness. Philip longed
for them also and his new life appeared to him unpleasant to bear. Later, however, the old people took an orphan
left by a relative, who had died of tuberculosis, into their
home and with her their life became less dreary. Philip,
too, found friends among his schoolmates. Besides, he
hoped that the time would soon come when neither he
nor his parents would seek consolation in anyone else
for they would join to live together in the parish which
he was certain to obtain.

And, in fact, he was ordained; he served as vicar; and
finally was promised a parish, in a remote village, to be
sure, but not at all a poor one.

But before he took over the parish, his parents died, one
following the other.

Philip Jaruga's heart became heavy. As long as his parents had been alive, their wishes and hopes had justified his becoming a priest without conviction. Seeing how happy they were Philip forgot that it was mainly for a good livelihood that he had chosen his condition, in which material thoughts ought to come last. After his parents were gone, this sole spiritual support in his new occupation disappeared. Only now did Philip see that he had thought of livelihood and position more for his parents' sake and that in the beginning something else seemed necessary for him. There came upon him a dreadful day of fear that he had irrevocably committed himself to a condition from which there was no escape. Though he told himself that it might be better to sever all bonds and leap into the world than to live in hypocrisy pretending to a zeal he did not have, he felt in his conscience that he could not sunder these bonds. For he had been anointed in God's name in the greatest confidence that he would go on to the end in the rank in which he had enrolled of his own accord in the fullness of spiritual and bodily powers. To flee seemed to him to be what every person regards as the greatest sin—seemed to be treachery. It also occurred to him that perhaps by deciding to become a priest he had already betrayed some divine decrees which had prepared him for something else in this world. But no matter how he kept turning his pitiful and disconsolate thoughts, it all came to one, that in such a case he would add a second betrayal to the first and that this would seem to be ridiculing the Lord. And as regards the Lord, it was like this. Every time Philip Jaruga determined to close his eyes to everything and be a priest without looking back, as fate had decided, he became the prey of religious despair, did not believe in God, and the priestly occupation seemed to him in this state of his spirit a chain of hypocrisy and wickedness. But as soon as he thought of discarding the cloth and becoming a lay person, he immediately experienced the conviction that God existed, that He was pursuing him, and that He was tormenting him with punishments and retributions for his deed.

So there was no possibility of turning away from the road he had chosen; moreover, just as he had formerly seen only that which a priestly career opened to him, now he could see only that which it closed before him.

And when he rode from the small station along the country road toward his new parish, he wondered in despair whether he should arrive there or whether he should stop, walk into a field and on this field somehow end it all. But he reached it, curiously observing on the way the locality where fate had appointed him to commence his holy and deplorable occupation.

Four villages comprised this parish: Malocin, Pamietow, Serbinow and Gawlice. The driver pointed them out along the way with his whip with the proud happiness that a person usually displays before a visitor in his abode and his neighborhood. The church was in Malocin. When they drove up before it, Father Philip saw a little, dark wooden church standing in drifts of yellow and rusty leaves sown by high chestnut trees. Out of similar leaf-drifts a little wooden parsonage emerged, equally darkened by age and fretted by almost bare branches of sycamores and ashes. All of this seemed to Father Philip an abode which was pleasant and awaiting him, but an abode which one comes to not every autumn but in the autumn of life for a long, quiet winter.

Sighing, he took possession of this house in common with an old aunt whom he sent for shortly.

Still, having found himself at the head of a populous parish and having seen all eyes turned on himself, he experienced what everyone who begins any work experiences.

He began to be concerned with carrying out his assignment well and effectively. He was led by the vague sense which compels a man to do well what he is doing. Even if for the time being one has neither enthusiasm for, nor faith in, what one has to do, out of stirring about the thing itself there develops something like enthusiasm and faith; afterwards there develop both happiness and especially hope that perhaps all this will be of help, will lead imperceptibly toward something more desirable. From the bells shaken by boys in little red capes, from the whiteness of the cloth on the altar, from the sun's glitter on the ampullas, from the power of his own voice whose every murmur during the mass resounded, despite his will, stronger, clearer and deeper than the bass pipes of the organ—from all of these there kept arising an unending pleasure which nourished Father Philip for some time and filled his life, especially since he was sustained by that which excites everyone into action; he was sustained by people's praise.

The former priest, who had died before Philip's arrival, had finally grown so old, weak and decrepit that, as people said, the sacristan, Anthony, all but celebrated the service for him, all but performed the marriage ceremonies. For what else could one call it when, during the last few nuptials, everyone saw that the priest only groaned leaning on a cane, while Anthony placed the stole on the hands of the newlyweds? The old rector remained fit for only one thing, to fleece people for spiritual services. To be sure, it was known in the parish that it was his housekeeper who did the fleecing, scraping up in this manner an inheritance for her old age. Before the priest's death it got so that she herself bargained about payments for weddings, christenings and funerals, bilking the people without pity or shame. But whether it was the housekeeper or the priest who was the cause of this greed, it all came to one, and people complained. After the young rector arrived; after his gray, meek aunt, who did not intrude into anything, settled with him; and moreover, since one now paid for everything, as before, only as much as one could afford—everyone was satisfied. The sacristan, Anthony, though he did not have the importance he had had during the old rector's time, but wishing to gain a new one, time after time repeated to Philip the words which were used to praise him.

For that matter, Father Philip himself had enough signs of his importance in the parish, and sometimes of an evening, being deprived of other temporal pleasures, he liked to count them over, to delight in them.

Once, for example, a poor man, a field worker from Pamietow, came to the church on a winter afternoon and, through Anthony, begged the priest to hear his confession as though he were begging for mercy.

At first Philip hesitated and almost didn't want to go. It was snowing outside and the wind was blowing; nor was it the time when he heard confessions.

He went, of course, and did not regret it later because the matter was important and confirmed him in his own importance in his post.

In the church which was already dark and only spottily lighted by Anthony's lantern, the peasant's shadow loomed, doubling, tripling and swelling on the walls. Bowing low, the peasant embraced Philip's legs so strongly that he almost lifted him, though the rector was a nearly huge man. Having done this, he briefly entreated for favor and forgiveness for his boldness, and then at the confessional, which swayed, knocked and creaked, waking echoes in the empty church—he explained the whole matter.

He had a wife with whom he did not get along well, so much so that he had finally left her, having found a certain girl and discovering through her that there was a joy in the world which he had never dreamed of. Theirs was a common-law marriage, but an exemplary one. They had children. But life is life and sin remains a sin. They had long wanted somehow to cleanse themselves of this dreadful guilt; they sought a way to dissolve the other marriage, since it sometimes happens that people from other classes, in the cities, for instance, dissolve them. And when recently, as the rector knew, a holy mission came to the parish, they both went to confession with a plea for help in this matter in the consistories of Their Excellencies, the bishops. Instead the mission fathers became very angry, did not grant absolution, prescribed a hard penance, ordered him to end his relationship with that Pelasia and return to his lawful wife. They even threatened the whole village with punishments which could fall on everyone because of this unheard of scandal. However, they both delayed because to part was for them like tearing their hearts with knives.

"But since then," the unfortunate from Pamietow admitted, "there's been no life for us on this earth.

"And people torment us more now," he continued. "For until there was no judgment things went along somehow. Now that there is the judgment of a Lord's servant everyone rails at us to do something about ourselves. Finally I said to myself, if that's how it is, I'll go to the rector and take what he says as holy. And if he orders me to do the same as the reverend mission fathers, then we will carry it out. Now I confess the sin that we did not do so at once, that we didn't obey."

The Pamietow sinner's tormented voice grated in the priest's ear and his warm breath moistened the priest's cheek.

Father Philip covered his face with his hand and one could not say that he listened without disquiet. Rarely did the village penitents give him such a hard question to decide. He was sorry for this stubborn and faithless man who was groaning out his grief. Quickly, however, gaining control of himself and recalling the definiteness of God's law in such matters as well as his brothers in Christ, the mission priests with whom he should hold—he confirmed their judgments.

The peasant kissed the priest's hands with full force as though he wanted him to know that he understood and that he was grateful for this fitting severity. A month later he returned to declare that he had fulfilled all the conditions of his penance, and, having received absolution, he thanked God and the rector that they had led him out of bondage to such a mortal sin.

Other minor events of life spun this incident over with forgetfulness, but the consciousness of it was in some way present in Philip's heart and, more than people's praises, gave him a feeling of being a true priest who could influence the lot of souls entrusted to him.

But the more he felt in his place as a pastor while carrying out his duties, the more he was drawn afterwards to the different life of ordinary people.

After each mass, after each rite during which he had the impression that he was swaying people's hearts and that he could carry them away wherever he wished with his words, after each such professional satisfaction, as it were, he wanted recreation; he felt a right to use his time as all mortals use it after work; he desired some reward. Consequently he began to go out among people, at first only after a christening or a wedding to gay family feasts; but after a time he went without seeking an occasion wherever he was invited, and he was invited not infrequently, for there were many households in the parish which were highly pleased if the priest visited them. All the more since the priest was good-looking and happy by nature, so that it was pleasant to tease him, to bring into the open from under the shelter of the priesthood the disposition of a young, robust boy.

Sometimes while Father Philip was taking off his worn everyday cassock to put on another, buttoned with silk buttons, before going out, he would suddenly be halted in these operations by the thought that if he had felt the call then he should confirm himself in it all the more by prayers, solitary reflections and some intellectual work in accord with his vocation. He even thought of one—a book about the Basilica of Saint Peter—spread piles of clean paper widely on his desk and bought the necessary books.

Whenever inclinations of this kind mastered him to such an extent that he did not accept some invitation and stayed at home, he was inconceivably sad afterwards. He would waste the evening on gloomy reflections and futile regrets, and the next day he would go to say mass as if he were going to be executed. So in the end he did not allow such scruples to affect him and whenever he felt like it, off he would go, even without being invited, where he knew one could drink and eat, laugh and play cards. In one or another manor house, at the farm manager's or the school principal's home there was always a little time for these things in the evening; half the larder and countless wines and homemade liqueurs were gladly spread before the guest.

At first the priest would demur; he suspected he could not take much alcohol.

"No, I've had enough," he would say, turning his glass upside down.

"Come now," the men would say. "What kind of priest do we have here, if he doesn't drink? The Lord Christ Himself transformed water into wine in Cana of Galilee. And at supper with the Apostles He didn't drink water, but wine."

"Then a cigarette, perhaps," others suggested.

No, he did not want to smoke either.

"Don't bother," the bolder ones interjected. "Father has chosen the third thing, the best of life's pleasures."

And if the festivity came after a christening, the ladies would fasten persistent eyes on his lips and say:

"If Father does everything as forthrightly as he christened that little one in church today, then bravo!"

"Bravo, bravo," cried the men, not having heard the

first words. "To the Father's health! This can't pass without a drink!"

In the end he would finally drink and after a while he drank and smoked as others did and even more than others.

He would also pay attention to the women, grasp their bare shoulders and, pretending outrage, exclaim:

"Woman, go home. Go dress yourself. Put something on those hands! Lead not to temptation."

He was anxious to be equal to pleasure, just as he had striven to be equal to his churchly obligations.

And though the matter of holy rites was thereby exposed time after time to jests and witticisms, he would think that even the holy was holy within limits, beyond which it became a human matter, more pleasurable to the heart even for being joked about. Besides, were people to regard his piety as so frail that any trifle could weaken it? Let them not think that!

Nevertheless, it was frail and there were many things which impaired it.

As months passed after months Anthony brought news to the sacristy ever less frequently about expressions of approval for the new rector; and Father Philip no longer felt the friendly curiosity and solemn readiness with which everyone in the church usually cleared his throat and sat up on seeing him as he entered to say mass or as he ascended the pulpit. He had already ceased to be someone new to the parish, someone to whom they flocked in order to see. There were not many things in him they wanted to penetrate. They already knew how he turned around at *Dominus vobiscum*, how he kneeled, how he folded his hands and how he incanted songs. They almost ceased to differentiate him from the altar, the pulpit and the confessional.

Father Philip began to lose patience and became agitated; during each divine service, during each confession, he waited for something which would justify these rites for him. For something which would unanswerably certify that he could carry this group of human souls upwards to God, that he could sway them, and that they could not get along without him. But the penitents only muttered commonplace sins into his ear according to catechistic patterns; the gay ones nudged one another and provoked one another to laughter, paying almost no attention to what was going on before the altar; those who listened to the mass seemed only to give themselves up passively to the ritual—nothing more.

The attention of people could compensate Philip for many worldly lacks in his occupation. Deprived of this incentive, and the more so as he felt it was not increasing, he began to be thoroughly bored at the altar and again worried about being a priest.

His modest fees for services also shortly ceased to be a novelty and, after some time, people began to observe that such a young priest in his first parish could be still cheaper. This one and that one would come to bargain; Father Philip was sometimes compelled to give in. Then he was tempted to recoup from other, more generous people; and in both cases he was always sad afterwards. When he made more it appeared to him that he had sinned; when he did not make enough he would—in his present state of mind—think:

"If I am not even to have a decent living then why

should I strive so and worry without readiness, without conviction?"

And he worried all the more because he had stopped visiting people; his time, except for the church and obligatory trips, passed in solitary sitting at the desk where, amid piles of clean paper, lay the sheet with the beginning of *The History of the Basilica of Saint Peter in Rome.* Sitting thus he envied the life of everyone who was not a priest; he was as if afraid to come near it. He was asked out as before, but he lacked the composure to enjoy himself which results from the proper carrying out of a service undertaken. Being a soured priest he was also becoming a soured man.

Once, however, he had to go to a church celebration. It was a big half-clerical, half-lay gathering; at the canon's dinner, dry meads and old wines were drunk. During this feast Father Philip involuntarily became gay, and from that time did not keep away things which, up to now, he had thought of as if they were a reward and rest after good work but which, it appears, could also be forgetfulness—after bad work. He not only did not keep them away but began to indulge without restraint. So much so that each day he did everything just to get it out of the way and right after dinner went somewhere to drink, to laugh, to play cards. Not infrequently too, it happened that when it was unexpectedly necessary to visit some sick person, Anthony the sacristan had to draw the quite tipsy rector away from the farm manager, the principal, or even from Czubaj, who had a store and a tavern. Anthony did this with a certain kind of sad satisfaction and along the way he would say to everyone he met:

"What's a sacristan, you say. But you couldn't do without a sacristan. You couldn't manage any priest."

It was just in this way that this same sacristan, Anthony, one evening pulled the tipsy rector out of the room behind the tavern, having made known that someone was waiting for him in the parsonage.

"Madam," he added, "told me to say that the rector's sister has come and that she is waiting."

"What sister," he asked astounded, walking unsteadily on the snow and hiccuping.

Then he entered not directly into his own room, but roundabout through the kitchen and his aunt's room, trying to sober up a bit in the course of this longer way. His aunt was, as usual at this time, already undressed and asleep. She slept apparently waiting for him, however, because she had left a lighted candle on a chair pushed a little away from the bed.

Father Philip bent over and touched the sleeping woman's shoulder.

"Aunt, aunt, who is it, who came?"

His aunt awakened and for a moment looked at him with the wandering, clouded stare not of this world of unexpectedly awakened old people. Next, having lifted herself, she said:

"Verosia has come."

"What Verosia?"

"Verosia—don't you remember? The one who lived in your home while you were in the seminary. She arrived here with such crying! Say something to her to stop her crying."

Father Philip passed to his room fighting the heaviness of hand and feet which was overcoming him increasingly and which was accompanied by a pitilessly aching pressure deep in his chest.

He stopped on the threshold of his room, holding onto the door frame, just in case.

On the lowest chair, in the corner between the sofa and the stove, sat a slight girl dressed in a small, frail navy blue hat and a thin coat unsuited for winter. She had stopped weeping but was rocking rhythmically back and forth as though, tormented by pain, she was attempting to mitigate it in this way.

Father Philip had not had much to do with this Verosia whom his parents had taken in when he had left home. On arriving for holidays he saw her little because in the mornings he was at the church and in the afternoons she went out to learn sewing. Nevertheless he recognized her now, though she was grown, for even then he had sometimes seen her bent over thus and rocking back and forth as if in painful musing. And having recognized, he recalled, in confusion, that his dying mother had told him to keep her in mind. He had kept her in mind when he was liquidating his parents' failing business to the extent of paying out the amount left her, with which she, it was said, set up a small millinery shop with someone. How else was he to remember, he a man bound by vows, about a lay person, an unrelated girl, actually. Yet now, as he looked, it seemed to him that he had not cared about her properly.

"Good evening," he said in his thick and slightly hoarse voice. She only lifted her head, as though she did not have the strength to rise. She did not appear either pretty or pleasant, only terribly wasted and as if seeking rescue.

"What is this? Good evening, Verosia," he repeated impatiently, not daring to approach himself from fear of staggering.

The girl looked a moment and suddenly, as though having experienced a terrible disappointment in her expectation of him, again began to cry. This sight sobered Philip considerably. He broke away from the wall, came up to her and placed his hand on her shoulder. He felt how the shoulder, shaking with crying, abruptly became motionless. She stopped sobbing and, it seemed, held her breath. Father Philip removed his hand, rubbed his face with it, stepped back, looked around, pulled up a chair and sat down at some distance. Then she began to sob again.

Father Philip mastered himself enough to renew his questions.

"Where have you been until now, Verosia? Why didn't you send word if things were so bad?"

Questioned from afar, she didn't want to say anything. Therefore they stayed that way a long time. He sat waiting for the alcohol to evaporate from him. She wept.

At last Philip rose and began to walk slowly in one direction and another until he stood just beside her. But he did not place his hand on her shoulder.

"Don't cry, child . . . child," he beseeched, as quietly as he could and his deep voice sounded like a distant, soft sigh of thunder.

Gropingly, uncertainly, apparently blinded by tears, she now reached for his hands and began to kiss them frantically. He pulled his hands away and jumped back as though it were the first time someone's lips had touched his palm. Immediately, however, he returned and clasping her head pressed it together with her hat for a split second against his chest.

"My hat," she whispered and pulled it off her head. A mass of light hair tumbled around her forehead and something like an imploring smile glistened in her wet eyes.

"I apologize," she breathed. "I'll tell everything later."

And she asked to be allowed to stay here with the aunt because she now had no place in the world where she could go. Fearing that she might begin weeping again, Philip did not ask any other questions and agreed to everything.

At first Verosia helped the aunt who could now barely walk and was very happy with such assistance. Soon, however, the aunt died and then Philip asked whether Verosia would not want to stay with him and run the house as an adopted sister. She blushed and said hesitatingly:

"If you want, I can do it. Until you find someone else."

No one else was found; moreover, Father Philip forgot all the things which had occupied him and tormented him up to now. He thought constantly only about Verosia's appearance and beauty. And not so much about her beauty as about the way she abided on earth. He kept recalling how she looked or how she wrinkled her forehead; with eyes closed he saw her agile, eloquent hands, or her strong, impetuous gait or, again, how she halted shyly in her walk, bending her head on her shoulder, as if ashamed by her own energy. He recalled with tenderness and with sadness everything she had said and done, as though these were unusual and, above all, irretrievable, forever lost events, which filled him with constant, insatiable longing. He could for hours recreate in memory that first evening when she appeared and sat in the corner with her bundle, weak and shrunken under the burden of a lot unknown to him. He could also endlessly be moved by recalling the moment when he once saw her, purple with strain, as she managed to halt a plunging horse in the yard. And whether he saw her strong, or weak and defenseless, he always saw her as he desired her to be. With every manifestation of her being, even the most contradictory ones, he was always solidly one; with all his soul he assented in fascination to everything she did. She could do anything. One thing she could not do—arouse other feelings in him besides the boundless fondness which it was not in his power to resist. He could usually resist the often occurring opportunities for amorous engagements. The ambition charging a man to have these among his assets is not within the range of priestly practices. Sparks did kindle but, allowed to lapse, they would die out, and, a while later, he did not remember them. But he could not resist putting his hand on Verosia's shoulder again. And having done this he asked again, as during the first conversation, why she had wept then. This time she held his hand fast, pressing it with her face against her shoulder and breathing quickly, as though she had been told to run, disclosed hurriedly that the one she had loved had left her. That when she had in confidence entrusted her affairs to him, he had quite simply robbed her of her savings which she had gathered renting a millinery store with another woman. Because of him she even had to give the other woman the rest of her money and then, left without a cent, took herself off. She was about to take her own life when she remembered Malocin and thought that the priest might not be mean to her.

The priest, however, was not angry but fell into dark despair. He covered his face with his hands and seemed to be shaken by sobs. He did not want to speak, and when

she begged him to say something, he said that he had not
expected that she already knew such things. She had to
apologize and swear to him that it had not been true
love at all, that on that evening she had cried more out
of shame. Since he kept pushing her away and despairing,
after a brief but difficult hesitation, kneeling and hiding
her head in his dark cassock, she admitted that from the
moment she had seen him that evening and from the
moment he had touched her shoulder, she saw only him
in the world and would ever see only him, even if Hell
was to consume her for it. Because she had liked him
without reserve from the first moment.

Pressing her rapturously to his chest, he whispered with
shame:

"I was drunk then."

"No," she denied emphatically.

"Yes," he said, not very conscious of what he was saying. "I was drunk with you. I am . . . with you . . . with
you. . . ."

Much later still, as if they had lost their senses, they
kept repeating imploringly with feverish lips:

"If it could only be thus for ages!"

From that time they burned with an unextinguished
and ever growing desire to cradle each other without end,
and Philip Jaruga was unaware almost of the world he
lived in. In church he did what he had grown used to,
but did it as though he were not present, returning constantly in thought and heart to the previous night with
Verosia, surprised that simple and same, it would seem,
loving joy could so grow and increase and vary.

Among the many admissions he made to Verosia, he
once said to her:

"I didn't know that there was such happiness in the world."

"I didn't know," he repeated and it seemed to him as though this had already happened, as though he had spoken or heard these words before.

Verosia was not only a paramour good for the first nights, but a person agreeable above everything else during the day and pleasant in prolonged living together. She was not one of those women who are always sought after by everyone. There was a type of man in the world, however, who, when he met her, was inclined to love her. When none of these was near her she waited patiently and humbly until he appeared. Toward all others she was modest and bashful and seemed not to be able, as they say, to count to three. She did not hunt anyone with glance or smile, but having once met her own she was transformed into a blaze, and it was just such a blaze that she now became. It was also part of her disposition that if she was not in love she tended to sit and rock in contemplation rather than be active. On the other hand, if she was contented with her nights, then everyday life absorbed her completely. She was contented with them now, so she hurried and stirred about the house all day establishing a new, charming order and a new management.

However, people were not contented with her. Formerly, when Philip used to worry that he was not worthy of being a priest, that he did not want to be one, when he offered mass with the greatest disinclination, the parish did not notice this in him and if it did, then only in a vague and approximate way, which had this effect that here and there it was said:

"He's no longer the same person he was."

When, though, one began to see him drunk, and especially when he began to drink at Czubaj's—not in the store it is true, only in the house, but still in a place where there was a tavern—that was already not a small offense. And the thing with Verosia, in everyone's opinion, completed the measure of this wickedness. That priests live with their housekeepers was not news to people; it belonged to the wisdom which his old parents had inculcated in him, saying that no one can jump out of the skin needing such acquaintance. Even children were, at worst, tolerated in such unions. But not to see the world beyond one's housekeeper, to neglect everyone and everything for her and only—it was said—to gaze into her eyes, to lie at her feet and to lead her about the orchard by the hand— to become the prey of such a passion, this was scandalous and forbidden. Moreover, it was said that she was in some way a relative of his.

Philip's and Verosia's love, unaware of these judgments, was meanwhile slowly ceasing to be an endless feast and becoming everyday food, not less but also not more.

Having regained his senses somewhat and looked around himself, Philip Jaruga felt worse in his priestly clothing than ever before. It seemed to him that it would not be hard even to crack rocks on the highway if someone only delivered him in exchange from his priesthood, of which he felt unworthy and in which he had not been able either to gain God's grace or to achieve recognition from other people. And his love for Verosia also now appeared to him as a terrible sin, with which the priesthood could not in any way be reconciled.

Embittered and already immersed, as he thought, in sins, he began to seek forgetfulness again in the glass—

and, as usual, when one reverts to evil, he began drinking furiously, as if possessed. Before long it happened that when some people arrived for a prearranged baptism the priest lay unconscious, and Anthony and Verosia barely managed to bring him to and lead him in; it was actually Anthony who completed the baptism, almost directing the priest's hand. Another time it happened that a coffin was about to be taken out of the church and one had to look God knows where to find the priest to officiate at the funeral.

What was worse, the priest when drunk spoke in a manner unbefitting to a man of the cloth. During the dance for the Fire Department he was heard prattling that if the Lord Jesus appeared in the world today He would soon be taken to a police station. At another time he complained about other priests, crying out that from hunger and war and such fools and hypocrites as there are among them, the Lord preserve us. It was amazing that he could speak so, being himself one of the worst. Once he even dared to speak insultingly about bishops, that who were they anyway, except that—he said—they wore cleft caps on their heads.

Finally it came to this that one day at daybreak he had to be pulled away to the mass from the manor house where he had spent the night playing cards and drinking. People going to work saw how Verosia, weeping, led him as he staggered. Where was she leading him, the shameless one; probably to bed when it was time, having got up modestly, to go say morning mass.

Then there were those who talked others into writing a complaint to the bishop. Many did not want to, for though they talked against the rector, they hesitated to join the complaint, saying:

"Why? A priest is fallible too. He does just as we do."

And feeling themselves sunk in similar iniquities, though they would have preferred another rector, they did not dare to complain.

The others, though, maintained that a priest must be different from all others, greater, better and holier. So finally the complaint was sent off.

Before the news of this matter, decided on in the village of Gawlice, reached the priest, he was standing in the pulpit one fine summer Sunday and reading the gospel of the destruction of Jerusalem. The lesson which he then drew from it laboriously was that the holy place of saints, that is to say, the church, should be venerated. That one should not within these walls, even though they were wooden and shabby, talk, behave improperly, push or laugh.

"If," he cried, "you stand almost at attention before a minister of state, a governor, that is all the more reason for doing the same in church before your Lord, before your God."

"Before your God," he repeated, striving to give his voice a solemn and thunderous sound.

His voice did not fail; it resounded powerfully. Philip made use of it with great pleasure. But the words which fell from his lips did not seem to move anyone.

The people were fatigued by working at the harvest and wearied by a riotous Saturday night.

The sluggish singing of the chorus, the dragging sounds of the organ, the smoke from the censers, the bright, beguiling peals of the ministrant bells; the priest's strong, resonant voice; and the sun slicing the church into strips of golden dust—all these put the praying parishioners into a state of blissful, torpid sleepiness.

Men holding candles, whose flames trembled from their breathing, had a hard time keeping their closing eyes open. Some of the women were kneeling, bent to the ground, with their foreheads almost resting on the floor in a humble yet rude posture. Others simply slept, not actually kneeling but rather sitting on their knees, with their heads propped against the walls of the side altars. One of the mothers set her little boy, perhaps two years old, on the steps of the altar and gave him a rosary to play with, which the child kept trying to tie around his fat, bare little leg. Another, a small girl, amused herself by lifting her dress to her chin and patting her little belly.

Father Philip saw all this first from the pulpit and then while turning away from the altar toward the church.

He saw and as of old could not at first contain his anger that these people seemed to be taking such a small part in the holy sacrifice which was taking place.

"Such people, they seem to be made of wood," he thought, passing from one side of the altar to the other.

And then, holding out his fingers to be washed by the altar boy, he fumed in turn at himself.

"What kind of priest am I, without power over their souls—and why did I push myself into this place which is not for me?"

Nonetheless during the *Agnus Dei* he became calm. He finished the remaining prayers mechanically, lulled by the loutish bleating of song to almost the same pious sleepiness as that of the parishioners sweltering in their thick clothes. And when, having turned toward them he announced:

"Ite missa est"

and they, having sung the last song, which was slowly fading away, began obediently to disperse, a thought arose in him unexpectedly: what did he actually want of them and of himself? Wasn't it they, wasn't it this multitude of people thronging the church like ants, wasn't it they who created these songs and these words which constitute the ritual and the customs and this whole piousness—and wasn't it they themselves who kept continuing them? And wasn't he needed here only so that people could fall into that heavenly and half-sleepy rapture which is for them a state of thankfulness, supplication and union with God?

He no longer wanted to affect his parish; he did not want to master or rule it.

Standing for a while beside the fence encircling the cemetery he watched sadly as they all went toward their homes in twos, in groups, down the sides of the hill on which the church stood. They were leaving without having any business with him; they were leaving him behind as though he had been delayed in some barren dissension. He was filled with longing for some help which would lead him out of it forever and it seemed to him that this help was somewhere nearby; he could almost feel that it had slipped through his hands, or crossed over his heart, but quickly eluded him like an unmollified mistress.

Before he ate dinner that day a peasant from Pamietow arrived to take him to a dying woman.

Returning home, later, around four, the priest dozed, for it was hot and the horses plodded slowly through the sands which here made up the road. His nap was interrupted by the loud shout of the peasant driving, who called out:

"Stop! Whoa! Get out of the way, why don't you!"

In the middle of the road Philip saw a ragged and tousled woman who was backing away from the horses and also shouting something. The horses stood still.

"What's happened? Who is that?" Philip asked, disagreeably affected.

"Why it's that Flos woman who went mad a year ago. When she stands in the road, she won't let you pass."

The strange woman began to shake her fist.

"Won't let you pass," she cried vindictively. "Look at him. You've gone mad yourself."

She came up to the priest and began to spread the numerous folds of her skirt.

"Oh," she said, "look, Father. The dogs in Gawlice tore my dress and that's why I can't show myself at home."

The horses jerked and moved ahead. The priest looked around, tried to find some coins, and saw the mad woman stick out her tongue at him. He became ashamed, but they were now some distance away from her.

Taking off his garments later in the sacristy and putting away the container with the Host, Philip asked the sacristan:

"Who is that Flos woman wandering about Pamietow? Who is that mad woman?"

Anthony turned his dull-yellowish head with its long, flat chin, on which there seemed to be enough space for still another face, toward the rector.

"It's true," he began carefully, as though feeling his way, "that she went mad some time ago, but she was always a little touched. Touched and not living well with her man. She went completely mad when that Flos beat her so that she lay senseless a good hour. He must have loosened something in her head."

The priest recalled vaguely that he had heard something about this incident in one of the houses where he visited. His face became flushed.

"He had stopped caring for his woman long ago," Anthony continued, folding the surplice and casting an observant yellow eye at the priest. "So much, that some time ago he took up with another girl, with Pelasia, and lived with her well, one might say. He had children with her. They lived together."

To the priest this story suddenly seemed ominously similar to something he knew well. And in the next instant he saw with enormous clarity the winter afternoon and the peasant, whose shadow loomed on the walls of the church.

He felt an unpleasant shudder go over his whole body. His legs became weak. He said, with an insincere, coarse laugh, as if, pressed to the wall, he wanted to squirm out of something:

"I know about that. He came to me for confession."

"That's so," Anthony took up. "It was just because of that that God's punishment came upon them. They went to the mission and that wasn't enough for them. They didn't want to believe in God's judgment. And when you, too, told them, they finally had to obey. It's clear though, Father, that that Flos received too light a penance, because God's finger touched him while he's still in this world. And though he returned to his rightful ties, he now has neither wife nor that girl."

"And what happened to that Pavlisia?" Philip asked, too loudly and with needless hauteur.

"To Pelasia," Anthony corrected. "Pelasia, though she was *that* kind, begging your pardon, Father, was a good girl and pious. It was she who talked him into going to confession. 'Go,' she said, 'God is compassionate. Maybe He'll let it pass. Maybe He'll permit us to have our happiness.' So stupid. It was then, as is known, he went to the mission fathers. And when he came back from seeing them, all he did was knock his head against a wall and want to take his and her life. Those who know them told how she begged him. 'Don't do that,' she said. 'Do as the fathers tell you.' She thought that if they did that perhaps God would figure out some reward for them. 'Maybe,' she would say, 'that woman of yours will die.' And later, when Flos went back to his wife, she left her children with some people, Pelasia, that is, and hired out as a harvest worker—not far, in Gawlice. But when her children, who lived with these people, died, she is said to have torn the clothes she was wearing and finally—when workers were being sought for France—she left. It was about three months ago. And so they all lost one another."

"She did well to go," Philip said and left the sacristy without turning toward Anthony.

"She did well," he repeated in a louder voice as he reached his room.

Outside it remained hot. During the trip back he had felt suffocated several times. Now he was glad to rest.

He looked at his four rooms, visible one after the other and glistening with the cleanliness that Verosia had caused. They were redolent of herbs and of wax.

"Verosia," he called. Only a slight quaver and silence

answered. That's right. Verosia had gone off for the whole afternoon to pick berries in the woods.

He sat down in a cane chair with arm rests and lowered his head on his chest, overpowered by an irresistible desire to sleep. And he must have fallen asleep for he began to see what seemed a small room in his parents' house. Everything was ordered in it as in those times: beds, a table, and chairs, only that there were no windows in the walls.

"But why did you wall up the windows?" he asked his parents.

"Why did you wall up the windows?" he kept asking, almost weeping. They seemed to want to answer, but said nothing. They seemed to be present, yet the room was empty.

Philip awoke from this sleep with an inconsolable sadness in his entire being. He spoke aloud:

"I don't know what to do.

"I don't know," he repeated with emphasis, "what to do."

Then he added, running his finger along the boundaries of the sun's reflection on the desk:

"I drove the children into the grave."

He whispered next the word "Satan" and suddenly, as if boasting sneeringly before someone who was worse than the evil, he avowed again:

"I did more. I drove the children into the grave."

He could not get over his surprise or comprehend that he had done so much harm to those people from Pamietow. He had tormented himself so about his lack of calling, his unzealous priesthood, his sins of omission, and here he had been the cause of the greatest misfortunes;

not then, but when it seemed to him that he best understood the loving severity of God's law and measured out justice according to it.

Like a drowning man, he now grasped at anything. He told himself that no matter what he would have done, he would not have saved these people from distress, that they would certainly have destroyed themselves anyway, and that the operation of the law had only bared an incurable decay; that it wasn't certain whether in this circle of events it was possible to avoid misery of one kind or another. But this defense was soon brushed away by the cruel certainty that the point was not what could or could not have been avoided but that he had not tried, that he had done nothing to prevent any distress of these three people, to make things easier for them in some way. That he was not thinking of this when he heard Flos's confession in the dark church. And always and everywhere—it wasn't this, this that he thought of. In his heart and his mind he had always thought only of himself, himself.

He kept sitting motionless and it seemed to him that he would never rise from under the burden of these Floses he knew so little, whose name he kept repeating from time to time—"Flos"—speaking in a quiet whisper—"Flos."

After some little time, however, without being sustained by anything and oppressed by lack of help, he unexpectedly felt the burgeoning within himself of a steadily growing happiness. It was as though the evil he had unwittingly brought upon Flos's family had finally drained all the evil from his own life. He had never felt as capable of taking life up anew as in this worst of all moments. He was no longer concerned with whether he should be a priest or not. Indeed, he could be a priest, now he could be a priest. This conviction grew within him with each moment, demanded disclosure—proclamation before the people.

"Today's Sunday. The sermon is already over," he thought. "God, why didn't I learn about this yesterday."

Feverishly he shuffled the papers on his desk. He tore the sheet on which the history of Saint Peter's Basilica in Rome had been started. He took another clean sheet and hurriedly began to make notes on it for his next sermon. For his first true sermon.

"And if it seems to you," he wrote, "that you have chosen the wrong occupation, that you will not persevere in your calling—remember that there is in the world one occupation, only one calling—to be good to another human being."

He crossed this out and began differently.

"To count one's sins, this is not life, it is decay. There is only one life and one calling. To help people. The world moves ahead not through the fulfilling of law, but through good deeds. . . ."

This seemed to him too difficult for the people and not entirely clear to himself. He crossed it out again and took another sheet.

"Whoever you are, priest, government employee, or peasant, you will accomplish nothing and not reach God without the love of man. For there is only one calling . . . one road to salvation. . . ." His writing slowed.

After a while he put his pen aside. He was dazed and didn't know what else to write. He wanted to rest, or at least to catch his breath. He got up before the window and opened it wider with a hand which did not seem to be his own. He even looked around in surprise, wondering whose hand he was seeing. The unprecedented disorder to which all at once almost everything about him gave way frightened him. Something began to pain him fearfully, but he didn't know what it was. Something writhed and struggled in his chest like an enraged animal. Something was also saddening him beyond endurance. He attempted to convince himself that this meant nothing, that he was standing on the threshold of nothing but happiness, on the threshold of a new life, which he was to begin at once. He felt the wish to lie down for a brief moment, but he was unable to reach the bed.

He was found lying on the floor, face down. Rescue attempts were made, but they could not help.

He was found by the sacristan Anthony who brought a letter from the diocesan curia summoning Father Philip to present himself and to explain the complaints made against him by the parishioners.

In a short time the parsonage was swarming with people. Verosia came back from the forest and, seeing the crowd before the porch, dropped the basket filled with berries and treading on the spreading black violet rills pushed her way through, amid the unfriendly silence of the throng, with a fearful cry: "What is it! What is it!"

When she was pulled away from the body she ran into the kitchen, grabbed up a knife and wanted to pierce herself with it.

After she was disarmed, she moaned:

"They killed him, killed him. They killed him, the bandits!"

And afterwards she cried out in utter despair:

"I wasn't—I wasn't with him!" She shouted so that she

became hoarse and fell into a faint. Outraged, they carried her outdoors to revive her.

"Not enough," they said, "that he died in sin. That Veronica still has to offend God in that way."

During this time the sultry and hot weather changed for the worse and just before sunset a storm gathered. The verdure, which had been yellow and gold before noon, now began to pale, darken and change color in the wind. Large dark blue and livid clouds lifted on the horizon. Shortly they paled and covered the entire sky with a uniform grayness and the earth with premature dusk. Lightning flashed and quickly thereafter there was a hoarse and sluggish rumble of thunder. In the next moment a thunderbolt hit with an explosive crash. The people went off to their homes. Word was sent to the authorities. Two peasants from the choir waited until the women came who were to dress and wash the rector. When the storm began to pass they walked up to the window which was reverberating from the downpour. After a while they saw through the turbulence of the bending trees a blaze in the distance, like an eruption of smoking, dark blood.

"Something's burning," they muttered together quietly.

They became frightened by the catastrophe spreading nearby and the death behind them. Not saying anything for a while, they gazed fearfully at Father Philip's face, which jumped out of the shadows whenever the lightning flashed.

Then turning toward the window they began to talk under their breath.

"The fire is in Gawlice," one of them whispered, "the lightning must have struck a building."

KAZIMIERZ WIERZYŃSKI (1894–   ), one of the out-standing modern Polish poets, has also written short stories and a well received biography of Chopin (1949), which has appeared in three languages. As a poet, Wierzyński has ranged in themes and techniques from exuberant youthful joy, to athletics—his *Laur olimpijski* (*The Olympic Laurel*), 1927, won him a first prize at the Ninth Olympic Games in Amsterdam in 1928—to meditations on his exile in this country. He now lives on Long Island and frequently publishes in *Wiadomości* (*News*), a Polish émigré weekly in London. His first book of short stories, *Granice świata* (*The Frontiers of the World*), appeared in 1933 and dealt with the first World War. A later book *Pobojowisko* (published in English as *The Forgotten Battlefield*, in 1944) contains accounts based on the Russo-German campaign against Poland in 1939.

JULIUS BALBIN, the translator, a native Pole, now lives in New York. He has published selections from Polish poets.

Patrol

KAZIMIERZ WIERZYŃSKI

$\mathcal{T}$he Hungarian regiment having been withdrawn for rest, we took over their positions on Uglenica. We cleaned out the trenches, repaired the barbed-wire entanglements, and emplaced our machine-guns. As fatuous military tradition demanded, we uncovered the mistakes of our predecessors at every step and saw at once where the fault lay, thus proving in all respects our superiority to those who had dug these underground structures with their own hands and had tested them on their own bodies.

The trenches ran through a wild forest, along a steep mountain slope which fell off abruptly. The Russians occupied the opposite mountain. The Hungarians had left us a shooting-range of some 1,300 yards.

It was April. In the morning we washed in water filled with husks of ice, and at noon the sun blazed in the sky.

There was no work to do. Now and then patrols were sent out at night. They would plunge into the dense dark woods crackling dry branches and an hour later would return reporting that all was well. Just that and nothing more!

On Uglenica, the war seemed idyllic: it was quiet, the air clear, and the scenery beautiful.

"Here I could live and love forever!" sang Lieutenant Siba in a falsetto voice on his first visit to our trenches. That tune, from a popular Viennese song, had become a sort of hymn for our troops. Siba was the officer in charge of mail; actually he kept busy ferreting out and spreading regimental news and gossip. For days on end, he would pass from trench to trench, spreading the fame of Uglenica throughout all the other units in the area.

From the mountain top unrolled a panorama as attractive as a poster of a Swiss resort. The trench-line climbed gently upwards, beyond the forest and around the other side of the mountain.

This sector bustled with traffic as though it were an officers' mess. From here it was closest to regimental headquarters, and here the field kitchen would first appear before dawn; here also our commanding officer resided in a large underground shelter.

He was a reserve officer, a genial Czech, with a cigar that never seemed to leave his lips, who obsessively kept filing his fingernails, and at noon would strip and expose his pocked skin to the sun. Captain Dolshak lived in ideal harmony with everybody. In his quiet, monotonous voice he would tell stories about hunts on the vast landed estates in Moravia where he had worked as a forester. Secretly he probably dreamed of being taken prisoner, the sooner the better.

The slope of Uglenica ended sharply near the commander's shelter and fell off in precipitous, many-storied ledges, making barbed-wire entanglements unnecessary. The trenches, like natural fortifications, stretched above the valley. A rolling terrain opened on an unobstructed view of the parallel chain of mountains slashed by the yellow scar of Russian trenches.

The expanse was so overwhelming that it brought a lump to one's throat.

Between the two mountain chains, the undulating earth suddenly piled up into a larger hill. It formed an amusing arc-like ridge that cut across the whole valley. After a short, steep climb, it abruptly fell back again. Amid the vast space all around us, it looked like a green-gray wall. At the foot of the ridge a few ramshackle peasant huts stood out fenced in by hedges—a desolate and deserted settlement.

On the map I found that the name of the ridge was Uschle Ramie (Withered Arm) and the settlement was Ptaszkow Wyzni (Eyrie).

I must confess that these names, so close to allegory and redolent of quasi-poetry, were not to my taste. Idyls—all right—but everything in moderation. If one finds new generations of lice under one's armpits every day, if every trench smells of socks, and if at night rats scamper across one's face, one's sensitivity calls for a different set of values. But our Swiss poster still did not have its fill of cloying sweetness and charm.

"We will have to shoot down those boxes," Lieutenant Ruth, our artillery observer said at one time, pointing to the huts.

Ruth would come to us frequently, bringing slivovitz and excellent cigars. This tall lumbering dolt was not popular in the regiment. Even at the front he did not shed the manners of a Viennese braggart. He played the part

of an ardent patriot and fooled himself with an unbearable warlike pathos.

His observation post lay hidden in a clump of spreading
pine trees, not far from the commander's residence. In
such terrain an artilleryman could operate just as easily in
the trenches, as had been done during the earlier occupation of Uglenica by the Hungarians. Ruth, however, chose
to move beyond the line and hide in the dense trees. There
he ordered a special wooden post to be set up and telephone lines installed.

His efforts were jeered at by some, but slivovitz and
fine cigars always managed to establish relations again.

About mid-April, the observer discovered something
odd in the terrain.

Between Uglenica and the opposite Russian-held mountain chain, at the foot of Uschle Ramie, a peasant was
plowing, as peacefully as could be. From afar, where we
stood, the horse seemed to move at a very slow pace,
while behind him the man seemed hardly to move.

"He's not worrying about the war at all!" said Ruth.
"He would be worth taking a pot shot at just to bring him
back to reality!"

Our artillery observer's discovery stirred up quite a
commotion around the commander's residence. We all
gathered around and looked at the unusual scene with
eager curiosity.

For several days the scene repeated itself without any
change. Having plowed through a small field close to his
hut, the peasant moved on to the very center of the valley,
and there, ridiculously small against the bare measureless
space, he threaded behind him a black strip of plowed
soil.

This super-tranquil scene, I must admit, made me impatient and angry. Such an exaggerated idyl was something unbearable. With a little sham and unction it could well have become a symbol of the Devil knows what! As for Ruth, he was upset by this inhabitant of Ptaszkow for another reason:

"Civilian trash!" he swore in German. "What a pig, jeering up in our faces like that! Here we risk our lives while that stupid fool over there thinks only of his filthy work! And who will guarantee that he isn't a spy?"

Our commander tried to soothe his anger in a really disarming fashion. He explained to him earnestly, though in a somewhat drowsy manner, that the thing furthest from the peasant's mind was to poke fun at his artillery, and that even if the peasant were a spy, he could do no spying from where he was.

However, the captain's droning voice failed to mitigate the artilleryman's anger.

"I'll shoot those miserable shacks to smithereens, I will!" he shouted. "I'll plow his earth in a way he'll remember till Doomsday!"

It should be noted that Ruth's slivovitz and cigars were of greater concern to us than his artillery plans. Sometimes at night we heard sporadic shots by patrols. Artillery we never heard at all. This sort of involuntary armistice meant something. Who would dare disturb it for any flimsy reason? This simple principle, adhered to on all fronts of all wars, could be grasped by all. We were sure even Ruth could understand it.

But when the peasant of Uschle Ramie began to plow up a third strip of land, the artilleryman became furious.

Rushing through the trenches, he sputtered an endless flow of obscenities and elaborate curses.

At length, he clambered up to his observation-post, from where we heard him bark orders to the battery. That evening fire was to be opened, and the fate of the Ptaszkow huts seemed sealed.

Unexpectedly, our commander found the right words to restore the artilleryman's composure. Stretched out half-naked in front of his shelter, he first expressed the supposition that Ruth would draw the fire of the Russians upon us; furthermore, he suggested, it would be a pity to stir up so much ado over a stubborn fool who promenaded his horse in front of the lines. But all this did not help: Ruth kept on raging.

Thereupon the quiet Czech, gazing at his polished fingernails, uttered in his monotonous, passionless voice:

"We would be put to shame before the Russians! Maybe they are as upset over that idiotic promenade as you are. But obviously the Russian counterpart of Lieutenant Ruth has more brains."

Ruth called off the order. Ptaszkow was saved for the day. The artilleryman left us slivovitz and cigars, fled to his battery, and did not show up in the shelter for the rest of the day. We ate and drank without him.

In the evening Siba came to our mess on Uglenica.

"What have you done to Ruth?" he asked upon entering. That was a rhetorical question since Siba knew everything. Bursting with laughter, he continued:

"That clown reported the whole incident to the colonel. He is storming against you and can't forgive you that 'spy.'"

There was no secret this officer in charge of mail did

not know. Ruth had managed to persuade the colonel that he should be given a free hand in firing at the terrain before our positions. This terrain had proved uncertain:

"Investigation has revealed the undoubted fact that the strip under purview fails to guarantee essential security in view of the intervening presence of physical structures . . . constituting an obstruction that, under given conditions . . . might afford comfort and shelter to said enemy. . . . Further, that said area has repeatedly revealed activities of civilian personnel with no assurance that such personnel may not be engaged in espionage. . . ."

The language of such reports was understandable to all of us. We knew the meaning of every single word and were aware, too, of the significance of the whole. Ruth had won—of that there was no doubt!

"He could not refrain," continued Siba, "from running after me with his report to dazzle me with his success. That rascal made a shrewd job of it. He will open fire tomorrow night—today you'll still have peace."

The trench tramp wandered on. We were left, I must admit, with a foolish feeling.

I was very young then, scarcely twenty years of age, but in the wear and tear of war I had lost, as they say, all needless sentimentality. I felt no regret about those old, dilapidated shacks, nor was I particularly moved by the fate in store for its inhabitants. What did trouble me was the thought that Ruth would achieve his goal. At the same time I was impatient with the calf-like calm with which those Ptaszkow peasants waited until his majesty, the artilleryman, would order their execution via telephone.

I turned to Dolshak.

"What's all this about, captain? Let me take a few men

on a patrol and give those people down there a warning
one way or another!"

"As you please! It's a bit late in the night, but I think
it should be done."

"Just to spite Ruth!" I added.

"Yes, for that alone!"

It was quite dark by the time I left the trenches with
a corporal and four privates. In the woods, the darkness
was impenetrable. Through the tree-tops seeped a dark
blue sky. Straight ahead of Uglenica, from behind the
Russian-occupied mountain, rose the moon, glowing with
a pale light.

We passed the sentinels and sank down a narrow passage a previous patrol had cut through. It was quite a
job tearing oneself free of the clutches of the needle-
sharp thickets, to walk along steep ledges in a tangle of
weeds and creeping plants, and to grope one's way along
a path one did not know and could not see.

I was sweating like a red mouse by the time we reached
the hump of the slope—a small clearing where patrols usually stopped and from where the Russian-occupied mountain stood out distinctly in its heavy contours, terrifying
there in the darkness, hostile and mysterious.

From where we were, a jutting promontory of Uglenica
hid Uschle Ramie from our view; the passage through
this mountain-fold offered even more difficulties. After an
hour's march, I cursed my idea, the patrol, Ruth, Ptaszkow, and Uschle Ramie. To hell with the whole thing!
Why should I be bothered by the mad folly of the artilleryman and by those few shacks lost in that infernal
valley!

We stumbled along like so many blind men. My corporal had lost his cap, and the faces of the soldiers were scratched by overhanging branches. Every now and then someone fell, cursing devilishly. At that point we would have offered an easy target to the Russians, had they spotted us.

The woods were thinning out at last, and reaching its outer edge, we threw ourselves on the ground behind the trees.

The moon shone high above the Russian positions, and the whole terrain seemed suffused with a green calm. The ridge now appeared unusually high, and the huts of Ptaszkow no longer resembled boxes and dilapidated structures. They now revealed to us the pitiful fruits of their owners' labors in the shape of shacks beneath ash trees, wells with cranes, fences, sheds, and heaps of potatoes covered with straw and sand.

This, then, was the settlement of the doomed. Here it was that Ruth's enemies had built their nest.

One had to admit that the tribe of Ptaszkow spies had certainly chosen their hide-out quite lightheartedly and improvidently. To cling to those Ptaszkow hills, to build their row of huts below them, on either side to expose themselves to the enemy—Austrian or Russian—all this struck one as far from well thought out or reasonable. It needs no metaphor to point out that all this was really playing with fire—the fire of any Lieutenant Ruth from either side!

It was delightful to stay there and rest for a while. I permitted the soldiers to smoke. We smoked cupping the glow of cigarettes in our hands. Meanwhile, I discussed the plan of action with the corporal.

He was to remain with two of the men at the edge of

the woods while I took the other two with me. We could easily make our way down the gentle mountain slope to the valley below, after which we would have to run over the flat terrain and take cover at the foot of the hills.

By the time we had finished our cigarettes, we imagined ourselves talking to the inhabitants of Ptaszkow when suddenly I thought of the actual purpose of our mission. What message were we bringing to these people? Lieutenant Ruth's threats and his sentence of death? An order to evacuate the terrain? A warning to save themselves from the savage anger of the mad artilleryman? Advice to escape from their huts?

No matter what message I might give those poor wretches, each one would ask me the question to which— damn it—I had forgotten to prepare an answer in advance!

Escape to where? Save and shelter themselves—where?

No sooner had I followed through this line of thought, and realized the monstrous foolishness of my plan, than I angrily smothered my cigarette.

I sprang to my feet. Simultaneously my ears were assaulted by a sudden blast.

A shell dropped. Artillery! A whizz and a boom! From where? A red flash sprang up amid the huts. Immediately there followed a second flash, a second boom—a third flash—then a fourth. Grenades!

"Russians," said the corporal.

Yes, the shells were coming from the other side. They were well aimed; they increased and soon were bombarding the whole settlement.

Fire leapt high from the flaming huts; the ash trees stood out stark in the successive flashes that flooded the ridge with light. From where we stood, the distant conflagration seemed not so much tragic as amusing, something like a luminous toy. I watched for people, but could see none. Maybe it was too far off, or maybe they had already escaped.

Escaped? But where to? The question recurred. Perhaps along that stretch of valley between the trenches—the remaining crevice along that front line—now nothing but a no-man's-land between two frontiers of death?

By now all the shacks had caught fire. A whole row of huts stood in flames along the illumined ridge—remote, entertaining and amusing.

And yet for a long, long time we could not tear our eyes from the spot.

"We should go back," advised the corporal. "Our men are lighting up the terrain."

Uglenica flashed with light-rockets. The front had awakened.

We were returning furious, breathless, and crestfallen. That was the hardest march, the worst patrol, and the most thoughtless expedition of my entire life.

No sooner had we reached the hump than Russian bullets whizzed past our heads. That topped it all!

Back in the passage we had to wait until the firing stopped. The artillery died down first. Ptaszkow could not be seen from there, only a fiery red glow in the sky.

I reached our trenches dead tired. In Dolshak's shelter, there was the usual commotion. Siba's sides shook with laughter.

"Wonderful! Ruth failed again! They snatched his fun from under his very nose. Let him report them."

Over our slivovitz, we discussed the unexpected attack

by the Russian artillery. I told about our patrol. Ptaszkow
was still aglow when word reached us that our battery
was about to fire on the huts. And before long we heard
Ruth telephoning from his observation post.

"Idiot!" exclaimed Siba, as we left the shelter.

In the rear from behind Uglenica, our cannon boomed.
Below and ahead of us, the shells exploded.

Six single shots. Then two salvoes! The Russians did
not return the fire.

The red glow remained in the sky throughout the
night.

The next day I met Ruth in the trenches. He had
brought a fresh supply of cigars and slivovitz.

With a malicious smirk he turned to me and said:

"They tell me you went on patrol to forewarn those
curs. But what did you intend to do with them? Evacuate them? To Uglenica, maybe? Bring that pig of a peasant here, along with his horse and plow."

He laughed heartily. We both laughed heartily. Yes, it
had been quite foolish on my part.

But the Swiss poster was disfigured beyond repair. The
bare and charred remains of the gutted settlement pro-
truded out of the valley.

From that day on, nobody ever again plowed the soil
of Ptaszkow.

". . . . In front of our positions, structures that might
have constituted objectives offering comfort and shelter to
the enemy were completely demolished, and the entire
terrain was cleared of civilian population, thus obviating
its use as a potential nest of espionage and counterintelli-
gence activities. . . ."

So, no doubt, ran Lieutenant Ruth's next report.

Only Siba kept insisting that in all his military career he could recall no better disposition of the troops and went on singing: "Here I could live and love forever."

MICHAŁ CHOROMAŃSKI (1904–   ) now lives in Montreal. It has been some time since he has been heard from as a writer, though a short novel *Biali bracia* (*The White Brothers*) was recently reprinted in Poland. Choromański is perhaps best known for his novel *Zazdrość i medycyna* (*Jealousy and Medicine*) published in 1932, which is widely known in Europe. The sixth edition of the Italian translation was published a few years ago in Rome.

THAD KOWALSKI, the translator, was born in Montreal, but shortly thereafter moved to this country. He has published a number of mystery and sports stories. At present he is employed by a governmental unit in Detroit.

A Cynical Tale

MICHAŁ CHOROMAŃSKI

J was as well acquainted with Engineer Tykiewicz as with his friend, Engineer Vavrzecki. On the other hand I did not know Eva Tykiewicz so well. As a rule the conversations which I had with her during my calls were laconic and uninteresting.

She would come forward to meet me, smiling artificially like a doll, and her opening words would be, "How well you look. The mountains must agree with you."

I would smile modestly and lightheartedly, crush my hat against my breast and answer, "Thank you, Madam. Of course, I feel better. Is your husband at home?"

Again we would exchange several meaningless remarks in the afternoon.

"I've been told that you intend to leave us soon. Is that true? May I offer you some cherry jam?"

I answered her and thanked her with a smile. Eva also smiled, oddly and artificially—one could suppose that she was really a doll.

We also discussed the weather and new books. The devil take them, but these conversations were very shallow and were totally inadequate grounds for understanding a person, especially when this person was Eva. Only once, I recall, did we broach a theme touching her life, but this happened after the catastrophe, when the events which are to be related were already behind us. We met in the first-class waiting room of the railway station. There was a sad expression on her face—it was clear that the experiences of the past months had completely exhausted her—but in spite of this she smiled as usual upon seeing me.

"Ah, it's you?" she said. "The mountains evidently don't agree with you, since you are leaving?"

I smiled darkly, near despair. As yet, I had not then admitted the whole truth. Instead of replying I heaved a deep sigh, but at first she did not notice this manifestation of sentimental emotion. Then, irrelevantly, she asked me a question.

"Do you know that the idea of good and evil is relative? Good, like everything else, can be feminine or masculine."

I denied this violently. I believed in the categorical imperative and the concept of good was an absolute to me.

"I tell you it is so," she repeated stubbornly. "When a woman says to a man, 'Will you be kind to me,' it must be understood that she wishes him to please her heart and soul. On the other hand, when a man says to a woman, 'Will you be kind to me,' it is as if he had said, 'Come to bed with me.'"

I exploded into half-witted laughter although my soul cried, "A lie! A lie!"

But all this occurred in August; the events unfolded

tragically and swiftly at the beginning of the summer. This was during the height of the season, when crowds of vacationers overran our health resort.

I had a small villa, or rather an ordinary peasant's cabin, situated on the slope of a green hill. My house creaked and trembled under the violence of the northwest winds; when the snow fell it sank to the eaves in the drifts. Through the windows I could see the town and mountains in the distance. Profiting from the isolation I spent the days like a primitive man. I walked around half-naked and sun-bathed for hours on the porch of my house. My only diversion was a secret and not very discreet observation of the life of my nearest neighbors—the Tykiewiczes and their friend, Vavrzecki.

The Tykiewicz villa, known as the Black Slates, was located nearby and below my veranda.

Every morning at eight o'clock I saw Mr. Thomas Tykiewicz come out on the terrace with a cigarette between his lips, in light-colored, checked pajamas, and ten minutes later, also with a cigarette between his lips and also in pajamas, came Mr. Jan Vavrzecki, with only this difference—that his pajamas were dark with light stripes. Both engineers put out their cigarettes simultaneously and turned to their breakfasts, with, one could say, ravenous appetites. First they ate a bit of cold chicken, then a dish of strawberries and cream, finally drank coffee with cream and again lit cigarettes. Shortly afterwards, however, the simple, healthy foods were replaced by sharp, moldy cheeses and cognac, in its tragic, morning appearance. But I will try not to get ahead of the story.

The engineers lay down in canvas chairs and did not arise until lunch. They almost never spoke. They were such close friends that they probably had no need for talk. Not until May did I notice that something seemed to appear to break between them. The first indication of this was that they suddenly became garrulous. Their animated voices could be heard discussing something continuously without interruption.

They were, all in all, a fascinating pair.

II

Thomas Tykiewicz attracted attention to himself mainly by his unusual ugliness. He was of rather short stature, fairly stout, with a thick, fatty neck, and the glossy bald skull of a dolichocephalic. He could be recognized at a distance of two or three kilometers by this shining baldness, sparkling like a reflector on a sunny day. He had an unhealthy, greenish complexion and large lips, which seemed swollen.

But it was strangely easy to become accustomed to Tykiewicz's outward appearance. He seemed to be very likable. Beneath the repulsive mask an attractive strength could be felt to which both men and women succumbed equally. Yes, it is almost unbelievable, but no one doubted his attraction for women. And to think that Eva chose this man for herself, to love in her way—morbidly. More than once I noticed the manner with which she watched him as we whiled away the time on their terrace. Her glance appeared languorous. Without a doubt, this was an irresistible animal love, an erotic entanglement. Later, Eva admitted it. Intellectually her husband did not overawe her at all. He was an electrical engineer, a sphere which did not touch her imagination. He had built a number of electrical works. She visited these contemporary, cubistic structures, examined dynamos, machines, and always departed with a feeling of slight disappointment. It was something else again where the works of the construction engineer, Jan Vavrzecki, were concerned. He was a bridge specialist, highly esteemed and famous in our country and abroad. When for the first time Eva saw a bridge built by him, rising like a half-moon over the abyss, she experienced a sensation of dizziness as if she herself were the bridge and that it was her flesh spanning the dangerous canyon. From then on she felt an affinity toward Vavrzecki.

Tykiewicz's friend was a Czech; he had, however, been brought up and had spent practically his whole life in our country. He was without distinction in appearance; he was neither ugly nor handsome. He was tall and he had luxuriant, wavy hair, the color of decayed straw. On the other hand, his face was so devoid of any distinguishing expression that everyone immediately forgot what it looked like. It erased itself from the memory like an unfixed snapshot in the sun. I am convinced that not even Tykiewicz could call up a likeness of his friend in his imagination. Once Tykiewicz half-jokingly said to him, "I was sure you were a brunet; it appears that you have yellow hair."

Eva quivered at these words and it seemed to me that she was a bit perturbed. Then, as if to conceal this confusion, she turned to me, "Perhaps you'd like some cherry jam?"

I have the impression that then, for the first time, I

felt a queer, slightly uneasy atmosphere dominating their terrace.

III

Anyhow, I was already predisposed by Richie. I recall that the day before a disjointed tale told by the boy impressed itself upon me.

It was toward the end of May. Vavrzecki had already lived for over a month with the Tykiewiczes. I was with them every afternoon for tea, but during the first four weeks I noticed nothing which would indicate strained relations. Only after the talk with Richie did it begin to appear to me that the atmosphere of mutual regard on the terrace of the Black Slates was superficial. I judged, however, that the boy had succeeded in making me believe it by his talk; he was truly a queer stripling.

The Tykiewiczes had an ancient cook who was also Eva's chambermaid. Her assistant and footman was the seventeen-year-old Richie. Powerfully built but very awkward, with the large hands of an adolescent, he always amused me with his odd behavior and the complete indifference with which he reacted toward everything happening around him. Everything was the same to him; whether the weather was fine or rainy; whether he was to have Sunday off or whether guests were expected. Why, he was even indifferent to his own well-being and health. Once, Eva noticed that Richie was swaying on his feet while serving. His face was red; his slanting, beery eyes burned unhealthily.

"Are you ill?" she inquired.

"I don't know," he answered indifferently. His mop of

black hair hung dolefully over his forehead. It was found that he had a fever.

"You must lie down."

"Very well," he answered, unmoved. If she had ordered him to run around the house all day long he would have done so with no less submissiveness.

He was always decently dressed in a black suit with a red, flashy tie, but nothing could induce him to wear socks and shoes and so he shuffled about the house in bedroom slippers or totally barefooted.

"You'll catch cold," I told him once. He looked up at me with his Mongolian eyes, but I had the feeling that in his God-like indifference he had not even noticed me.

"Maybe I'll catch cold," he echoed.

A wind arose and a rain cloud came overhead. The striped awning over the terrace billowed; the first drops of rain fell noisily on the roof. It became dark and after a moment two thunderbolts struck violently above us, like a cannon salvo. I was startled and reacted by jumping for the door. Eva's voice echoed in the corridor.

"Oh God, what's going on?"

Tykiewicz, in pajamas, looked through the door, startled by the storm. Richie alone stood completely serene in the middle of the terrace and mumbled something under his breath.

"Roll up the awning," Tykiewicz commanded, "and shut the windows."

"Very well," Richie agreed apathetically. He went out on the steps, climbed on the railing and, standing under the torrential downpour amid thunder and lightning, fiddled with the awnings. After this, without hurry, he circled the house and closed the windows. When he returned to the veranda he was soaking wet but still indifferent, and it might be said, somnolent. The water poured from his bare feet. He went to the kitchen, leaving behind him a trail of wet footprints.

I will admit that I could not understand why the Tykiewiczes retained such a servant. I once remarked on this to Tykiewicz but he remained silent, as if reluctant to answer. I reconciled myself to this state of affairs and disregarded Richie's actions, just like everyone else.

His most amusing trait was his constant humming and mumbling under his breath. It is true, he did this only when there was no one in the room, but there were times when he apparently forgot himself and suddenly began to hum loudly and melodiously in front of everyone. At first I would start violently, appalled; later, I grew accustomed to these strange manifestations of musicality. None of us even laughed when suddenly, at a most inappropriate moment, the stifled, strange sounds burst over our heads.

On one occasion I came to the Tykiewiczes but found no one at home. I was about to return home when I heard a rustle in the living room. I looked in through a terrace window. Suddenly something tinkled noisily, then crashed. I saw that Richie stood beside the piano in the living room mumbling to himself. I waited for what was to come. Richie held both his palms on his red tie and with great dejection stared at the keyboard. His childish face was, at that moment, dark, as if covered with black down. Suddenly he stretched out his right hand, hesitated for a second, and then struck the white keys full strength with his fist. The piano groaned. Richie closed the lid and glanced around. We looked at each other in silence.

"Have you gone mad?" I said.

"I was dusting," he answered, abashed.

The lie irritated me and I wanted to give him a dressing down but Richie was again apathetic and disarming.

"How can Madam play on this?" he indicated the piano with his hand.

This struck me as odd and a somewhat absurd thought crept through my head. "Eva?" I asked.

"Yes," he answered dreamily.

I thought, "This lad is a strange monster," still under the influence of the notion which dazzled me. I was sure that even the boy understood me. From that time on I could not rid myself of the feeling that we were fellow conspirators. This did not please me and I lived in constant anger at myself, particularly after Richie's first visit to me. I talked with him then at some length and that conversation stuck hypnotically and annoyingly in my memory.

I was sitting on the porch, smoking a pipe. It was evening. With one eye I observed the sunset; with the other I looked at the black roof of the Tykiewicz villa. Everywhere there was such luxuriant grass that even the path leading to my house was overgrown by it. This evening the mountains appeared to be especially close; the air was blue and clear. I sat like that for an hour while the sun succeeded in hiding itself behind a peak, but it was still quite light so that I could plainly see Richie clearing the table on the veranda. Then he disappeared and the two engineers came out on the terrace. From there on I ceased watching the sunset and looked at them. Vavrzecki wore pajamas, while Tykiewicz was clad in flannel sport clothes and a large straw hat. I thought he was preparing to go into town. They smoked cigarettes while leaning against the railing. Vavrzecki was saying something in a low, monotonous voice. I heard Tykiewicz interrupt him with an exclamation, "God be with you!" then clap him on the shoulder and quickly run down the steps. I saw him walking down the highway for some time; he held his hat in his hands and his bald pate shone in the sunset's light like a reflector.

The other man was left alone on the veranda and watched Tykiewicz for a long time. Immediately beyond the veranda, that is, at the rear of the villa, were the kitchen doors. They had remained shut. I knew, therefore, that no one besides Tykiewicz had left the house and that is why I was so unpleasantly startled when the grass parted below me, undulated suddenly, and Richie appeared noiselessly from behind a bush.

"Where the devil did you come from?" I shouted.

With his bare foot he kicked a dry branch aside and then with an ungainly but agile movement clambered up on the path and stood before me rigidly. He appeared to be somewhat perturbed. There were stalks of grass in his hair and on his shoulders; he held his hands to his throat as if he were being choked. I reflected that now he would mumble something as usual and was prepared for the oddest sounds, but this time he spoke like a human being.

"He hit her."

This was so unexpected that I was startled. "What do you mean?" I demanded.

"He hit her with his fist," he whispered and fixed his eyes on the ground.

I guessed the trouble immediately. "Go on, go on," I said gently. I was proud of my knowledge of human psychology. I therefore prepared to hear out a long tale from the boy, whatever it was going to be. "I am curious," I said to myself, "who, according to him, hit whom? Maybe Tykiewicz has beaten the cook?" I nearly choked with laughter.

Richie constantly kept yanking his tie. This was the only thing which betrayed his agitation. He then looked around, glanced at the terrace of the Black Slates where Vavrzecki stood motionless, leaning against the railing, and answered in a thin, boyish voice, "I—am—afraid—."

This surprised me. This indifferent, simple child, unable to profit by experience, nevertheless evidently felt something both disagreeable and frightful. But even for this I managed a psychological explanation. According to my theories, the case properly rested on the fact that this callow boy, possessing fantastic, childish ideas, had, from time to time, something in the nature of a hysterical hallucination. He had probably imagined some incredible occurrence and frightened himself with his own phantasy. At any rate it was interesting.

"Now, now," I said soothingly. "You must have had a horrible dream?"

He looked at me reproachfully. "Why do you say that, if you understand?" he whispered.

I flushed violently and my pipe went out. "Don't wander around idly," I replied and struck a match, "otherwise we will soon have to put you in an insane asylum." But the boy made no move to leave. "Away from here!" I shouted.

To get away Richie took a backward step but hesitated and began to stammer something unintelligible. I understood nothing of his prattling. At last I made it out. "He hit Madam Eva with his fist!"

"What!" I cried, and forgot to put out the match.

"He hit Madam Eva," Richie repeated.

"Who?"

"Mr. Vavrzecki," and without glancing behind him Richie used his elbow to indicate the direction to the house of the Black Slates.

This was beyond all belief; this I could not comprehend at all. "He must be lying!" I thought.

"How did it happen?" I asked in an attempt to get to the bottom of this mysterious affair.

"I was cleaning the corridor," the boy said, "and they were at the end of the corridor, near the window, he and Madam Eva. Then he said something to her and suddenly hit her on the arm with his fist."

"You're talking nonsense," I muttered. Shamefully, I must admit that for a moment I believed this trash. To that extent did I succumb to the boy's mood. The quickly falling night suddenly appeared to be gloomy and suffocating. "The devil knows what you have fancied," I continued without conviction and immediately tossed the match away with a shout; it had managed to burn my fingers.

I rose to go into the house. Again I heard Richie's voice behind me. It was changed—hoarse.

"I—am—afraid. Things are bad in our house."

His fear imparted itself to me partially but I overcame it easily. I turned, and said sympathetically in farewell, "What are you afraid of, you scamp?"

When I turned around I was shocked to find him gone and out of sight. He had disappeared, the devil knew where, and only a branch of a bush still quivered momentarily. "A foolish trick," I thought. Then I calmed down. "The poor boy!"

A garden lamp was lit on the Tykiewiczes' terrace, but Vavrzecki continued to stand motionless against the railing, smoking a cigarette. I saw that Richie had fetched the lamp out on the terrace. "He moves as silently as if he had wings," I thought with distaste.

IV

Nothing strange, then, that on the following day I was still disturbed by this small adventure.

At the Tykiewiczes, during tea, I watched everyone furtively but saw nothing unusual. Eva sat in a deep, canvas chair, holding a cup of tea on her knees and a large Chinese fan in her right hand. A black shawl embroidered with green peacocks hung from her shoulders with the tassels on the floor. Her head was bowed on her breast as if she were minutely examining the cup. Her usual smile was playing across her face. However, she raised her head momentarily in slight confusion. This occurred when Tykiewicz tossed a pleasantry in Vavrzecki's direction while walking the length of the terrace.

"Just today I proved to myself that you are a blond. I thought you had dark hair."

The other did not answer. He sat beside me, silent and out of reach, paying attention to nothing.

Tykiewicz wiped his bald cranium with a foulard handkerchief and again began pacing back and forth. For some reason I felt sad. I recalled yesterday's conversation with the boy and decided to repeat it with suitable alterations, of course; but before I was even able to open my mouth something twanged frighteningly over my head like the snapping of a piano string. I turned, displeased.

Richie stood over me with a sleepy look, serving the cream.

"Somehow I cannot get used to you," I said sourly. My annoyance increased when I caught his wink which decidedly signified the wink of a partner. I settled more comfortably in my easy chair and thought, "What are you thinking of, you sniveler? I shall relate everything immediately." But angrily I realized that I would say nothing, that I would not even stammer out a word. The boy then disappeared.

"You were about to say something," Eva remarked.

I denied it politely. I merely mentioned, ironically, that it seemed to me that Richie had been ill since yesterday. Who could tell whether or not this lad was normal. I intimated this very diffidently, in spite of myself, but my statement created an unexpected storm. Everyone literally threw himself at me as if I were some kind of blasphemer. Even Vavrzecki added that I had an unjustified antipathy toward the wretch. He was, in spite of everything, the most agreeable and most able lad on earth. This exaggeration angered me.

"You misunderstood me," I began, but Tykiewicz interrupted me. He patted his bald pate with exasperation and ran back and forth.

"I am convinced," he practically shouted, "that there is no more devoted creature in this whole world. This must be cherished."

"But I have no doubt of it, my dear sir."

"No, Edward," Tykiewicz taxed me again, "if you were our age—if you were forty—you would realize what rare things friendship and affection are in this world!"

I was even more confused. "And Tykiewicz says this to me?" I reflected. "He who is so fortunate with people and who has a friend like Vavrzecki?" I know now that my suspicions were not without justification. Despite this I managed a protest.

"I don't know why everyone throws up my age to me," I said bitterly. "The same thought may be born in the mind of a man of twenty-odd as well as in a dotard, for ideas have no age."

At this Vavrzecki attempted to prove to me that ideas do have ages; they are born and they wither—like humans. They are bound to the biological process of the individual. "Ideas of love and affection are no more than twenty years of age," he concluded. "After thirty they change into agreement; after forty they are replaced by a notion of comfort."

"Ah, yes," Eva replied, without raising her head. Tykiewicz paused, glanced at her and then at Vavrzecki. Vavrzecki returned this look with a smile. However, I felt a bit too provoked to permit myself to observe those around me quietly.

"I am sorry that you gentlemen speak to me as if I were a child," I replied, offended. "I ceased believing in human friendship and affection a long time ago. But it seemed to me that you gentlemen subscribed to an opposite belief."

"Bravo!" Eva turned her face toward me with interest and her lips trembled encouragingly. I was delighted by her, objectively and completely. Her approbation gave me the incentive to go on.

"As far as love is concerned," I cried, enraptured, "I have not lost faith in it and I also believe in the existence of absolute goodness. But alas! women are better attuned to these feelings than men."

As I recall it, my youthful naivety and ardor created consternation. But in the meantime I was proud that no one laughed and I was convinced that I had converted them. I did not notice that they attributed a different meaning to our conversation which I had steered onto dangerous ground. Tykiewicz came up to me with false heartiness and began, "Edward, Edward . . ." but I brushed him off with a gesture.

"Still, I don't understand," I went on, "why a remark about Richie should assume such a universal and sublime character. I can prove that this boy is a trifle abnormal."

I nearly committed a folly and with enthusiastic delusion was about to divulge everything. Fortunately, or unfortunately, I noticed the serving-boy standing in the door. Before my eyes he grew on the threshold like a fakir's palm tree in a flowerpot. I stopped short, not knowing whether I should be angry or grateful. And then I noticed that no one was paying me any attention. Something occurred which I could not unravel. Tykiewicz strode in the direction of the stairs and stood with his back to us. He wiped his fleshy, greenish neck and bald head continuously. His thickset, odd figure created an unexpected reaction within me; I felt something akin to pity for him. Instinct told me he was unhappy. But most of all it was Vavrzecki who surprised me. He sat beside me, his face flushed to the degree that he nearly had tears in his eyes. "What's wrong with them?" I said to myself. Only Eva smiled serenely and with good-fellowship—like a nice, kindhearted doll. We remained silent for a long while until at last I could not endure it and, bowing clumsily, I left. I was already on the path when I heard quick footsteps behind me and a voice called.

"Edward! Edward!"

Tykiewicz caught up with me.

"Why'd you leave so suddenly?" he asked, catching his breath with difficulty. "One would have thought you'd been angered by us." He looked at me, ugly and yet attractive. I realized that it was at such moments that he could be attractive to women.

"Sir," I said with dignity, "I was certain that my tactless comment regarding the conduct of your servant angered everyone."

"Bless you, lad," he said, "no one even thought you were speaking of Richie."

"Really?" I asked emphatically. Tykiewicz sighed and released my hand which he had been holding.

"I received a telegram about a serious matter concerning an electrical installation which I have built," he remarked. "That is why we were all upset, as you noticed. We are awaiting a second one."

I was certain he was lying. But I pretended to believe him.

"I noticed nothing, but now I understand," I retorted.

V

I really had understood nothing for within an hour,

more or less, a letter carrier with a telegram rode up to the Tykiewiczes on a bicycle.

"You see, another telegram," Tykiewicz shouted to me, and a note of triumph rang in his voice.

I nodded sympathetically. Tykiewicz was excited and restless. He really must have had some kind of mishap. I had to confirm this, feeling that the life of the people living at the Black Slates was beginning to concern me more and more. Therefore, toward evening as usual, I took up my observation post. The two engineers again stood on the terrace, smoking cigarettes. Tykiewicz was on the verge of departure, for, like yesterday, he was holding his hat in his hand.

"Certainly, I must go," he said loudly to his companion.

"I advise against it," Vavrzecki answered. "You can see how badly this is all going."

I thought they were speaking of a machine at the power plant. This was evidently so for they continued to repeat, "She is out of order." Tykiewicz even remarked, "I would never have suspected it. Everything seemed to be without fault."

But his friend cut him short suddenly. "Don't talk so loudly; she's coming."

Who was "she"? This could not be the machine. Aha! I suppressed an outcry with difficulty when I saw Eva come on the terrace immediately after Vavrzecki's warning. She too had probably heard the last remark for she inquired, "Who are you talking about? Who is coming?"

"The power plant," Tykiewicz answered, fanning himself with his hat although the evening was not at all warm.

I was taken aback and rebuked myself for my suspicions. I was certainly seeing things which did not exist.

But in spite of this I continued to watch the action on the terrace. I saw Eva disappear again into the house and Tykiewicz, bidding his friend good-bye, waddle in the direction of town. Vavrzecki remained on the terrace. He was like a column of stone and from time to time made vague motions with his hand, shaking the ash from his glowing cigarette. Night fell swiftly. After a few minutes I could barely see the white outline of his figure and the blot of his face. And then Eva came out on the terrace with a garden lantern in her hand. She stopped beside Vavrzecki and set the lantern between them on the balustrade. Vavrzecki's clothes became yellow and the rays fell on his face. I could hardly see Eva. She wore a black shawl; her face was shaded by her dark hair.

I had a sudden presentiment that an interesting and disturbing scene would occur between them immediately. The premonition angered me. "I dream of horrors, like the servant," I thought, but nevertheless something rooted me to the porch and forced me to continue to watch. There was a certainty which suddenly grew within me, a certainty that Eva was threatened with something disagreeable and that I ought to remain to come to her aid, just in case. Immediately I felt justified in my indiscretion and from then on I watched them without scruple. An odd pantomime was taking place on the terrace.

Vavrzecki took a step backward and threw the cigarette far away. It arched and fell out in the yard. Eva slid an arm from under the shawl—I saw the curve of her shoulder—and extended it in Vavrzecki's direction. But he moved back another step and lowered his head as if he were bowing. Eva moved her hand in the air as if to catch his sleeve, although the distance between them was

71

a bit too great for that. Vavrzecki continued to back away and was already in the shadows near the door. Then I heard a stifled cry.

"Don't run away, at least not today."

Eva's voice was almost unrecognizable; it was dry, commanding, and, at the same time, full of pain. Vavrzecki mumbled an answer but soon came out of the shadows and returned to his place near the balustrade. Thanks to a wind which rose up I heard every word. Eva's low, beautiful alto especially rang out in the heavy silence.

"It is by no means easy for a woman to talk about it," Eva said. "I have felt out of sorts with myself since yesterday afternoon. I don't know who is to blame, you or I."

"It's unfortunate that you don't know," Vavrzecki answered and again lit a cigarette. Eva made an impatient motion.

"It's all the same to me," she said. "I can't live any longer in such an atmosphere and I will not live in it." Then she asked, "Why do you run away?"

"Oh, come!"

"A stranger would think," she continued, "that your running away is contemptible, but you know very well that you run to humiliate me. That is gross baseness."

In answer I heard a grumble or a sigh.

"Oh, you mustn't think I am greatly upset by it," the woman's alto rang. "We women have only that value which is placed upon us by men. It's nothing strange that I become mean in your company!" She exploded into such an unpleasant laugh that at first I thought she had succumbed to tearful hysterics. Then she continued, a bit more calmly. "If I harass you it is your own fault because you provoke me."

"I can leave," Vavrzecki answered.

She laughed. "Running away again? Nevertheless, I don't believe you would—you're afraid of Thomas." Vavrzecki made a violent gesture with his hand. "Oh, don't protest. I am convinced that if you have any feelings toward me you stifle them, not in consideration of friendship but because of cowardice."

"My relations with Thomas will not change because you doubt him," Vavrzecki replied, almost impolitely.

"Indeed, they could change," she said.

The darkness became thicker. A moth flew around the lantern which threw two strips of light on the grass.

"Mr. Vavrzecki," Eva said, "do you recall the day we became acquainted? It will be nine years in October. I know that you had then arrived from Prague only to advise Thomas not to marry me. You were wrong then, as I did not betray my husband even once—but now I really will betray him!"

She rearranged the shawl about her and sidled so quickly to Vavrzecki that it seemed to me their bodies touched.

"I'll betray him with you," she said.

I felt a constriction in my breast. The white figure of the engineer backed into the shadows of the terrace but after a little time it emerged. Suddenly Vavrzecki raised a fist over his head. I could not discern the expression on his face; I only saw his brows flow into a continuous, black line. I jumped, but I did not have time to take a step when a fearful clatter resounded in the Tykiewiczes' home. I thought someone had fired a gun. I froze in my tracks, not knowing what to do. On the terrace Vavrzecki and Eva had apparently lost their heads also. Vavrzecki lowered his fist and turned slowly toward the door. Eva too, glanced in that direction. I heard Vavrzecki say, "I don't understand," but Eva had already run past him and gone in the open door. She returned immediately.

"It seems Richie broke the dishes!" Then they both entered the house. For a long time the garden lantern continued to burn on the terrace.

VI

Events continued ever faster.

The next day, early in the morning, Eva passed near my shack. I stood at the window.

"I'm going for a stroll," she shouted to me. "How do you feel here in the mountains?"

I thanked her and laughed helplessly. She seemed to be paler than usual, there were shadows under her eyes. But she also laughed affectedly, like a doll, although her eyes remained dignified and steady. She crossed the path and soon disappeared into the wood.

After a moment I heard the slam of a door and Richie dashed out of the kitchen. Leaping over the bushes, oblivious of the weeds, he followed her trail. I felt ill at ease as I had lost all faith in the lad.

Punctually at eight Tykiewicz came out on the terrace of the Black Slates, with Vavrzecki following a few minutes later. The cook served them.

"Where is Richie?" Tykiewicz asked.

In reply the cook began to grumble and complain about the damned boy who always kept disappearing before her eyes like a cloud.

The men consumed their usual breakfast—cold fowl and strawberries. Now, I thought, they would be silent as always, but Tykiewicz said, "I will leave—and today."

The other advised against it. At this moment I saw a cyclist on the road, riding in from town. This was the letter carrier with yet a third telegram. Tykiewicz accepted it but did not deign to read it. It was plain that even Vavrzecki was not at all interested in its contents. But I was even more surprised when I saw Tykiewicz crush the telegram in his hand and throw it away on the floor without looking at it. Plainly, he had either known its contents beforehand, or else he was totally indifferent to it.

I don't know what went on after that for the carrier came to me with a letter and a money order from my father. After he left I noticed he had forgotten his pencil. I went down the stairs and returned it to him at the moment he was mounting his bicycle. Returning I had to pass near the Tykiewiczes' terrace. Its left side was hung with an awning, therefore, by stopping beside it I could be sure that no one would see me. Thus, I found myself about two paces away from the speakers. Tykiewicz was talking.

"When a woman ceases to love a man she begins to notice all his moral and physical imperfections to which she had paid no attention up to that time. For example, yesterday she noticed that you have beautiful hair—I heard her tell you so—therefore I reminded her of it, casually. I know that at the same time she noticed I am bald, as if she had been unaware of it for the past nine years."

I did not know whether he said this with sorrow or with sarcasm.

"I know now that for almost ten years I have lived under the same roof with a complete and unfriendly stranger," he went on after a pause. "The worst of it is, that all my plans have gone awry. This isn't just a crippling, it's an evil visitation. It creates a thousand-volt tension; the only thing lacking is a notice, 'Danger! Do not touch!' "

Something squeaked on the terrace. Tykiewicz had probably sat down in the reclining chair.

"I've guessed why you want to leave," Vavrzecki said, "but do I understand correctly why you leave me behind?"

"But God be with you!" Tykiewicz cried out; the other man interrupted him.

"Can't you really see any other way out? Wouldn't it be simpler to leave and disappear? I'll help you get away."

"It's impossible," Tykiewicz began. "I feel like a complete prisoner. The only way out is—"

The terrace door clicked. I heard footsteps and then Eva's breathless voice. "What's happened?" she asked.

Apparently a moment of confusion followed. At last Tykiewicz answered quietly. "Nothing. Why should anything have happened?"

"But you ordered me to return home immediately because you wanted to see me."

There was the sound of coughing, like muffled laughter.

"But you did summon me," Eva repeated.

Tykiewicz protested. "Summoned you? Nothing of the sort."

"That's strange," Eva said, suspiciously. "Then why

did Richie follow me into the woods and beg me to return immediately because you were waiting for me?"

"Probably another one of his whims," Vavrzecki replied. Before I could retreat he had raised the awning, looked out, and saw me standing there below the balustrade. "Ah, so it's you?" he said, sorrowfully.

I blushed and stood openmouthed. But he must have been preoccupied with something else for he did not notice my confusion. I greeted them and entered the terrace. After yesterday's scene, to which I had been a witness, and today's overheard conversation, I felt uncomfortable. Luckily no one paid any attention to me.

Eva stood in the center of the terrace, wiping the corners of her mouth with a coarse, nervous movement. Her handkerchief was completely smeared with red lipstick. Vavrzecki remained half hidden by the awning. With searching glances Tykiewicz looked all around himself. Then he noticed something in a corner, on the floor, and he twisted impatiently in his chair. After a moment, he rose and began to pace back and forth over the length of the terrace. From time to time he stole a glance into the corner and his irritation increased. It appeared to me that his pacing was an attempt to get near the corner and move the obstructing chair from there. At last he reached his goal and shoved the chair aside with his foot. He bent down quickly and picked up something. He then became tranquil and holding something in his closed fist, moved closer to Eva.

"Of course, I wanted to see you," he said, anxiously. "I received a third telegram," he opened his fist and handed the crushed telegram to his wife.

She read it aloud. " 'Presence required immediately at

building site.' Then you really must go?" she said. She glanced at Vavrzecki. "And you too?"

"No," he answered drily.

Without reason, Eva burst into laughter. This laugh, disagreeable and unnatural, recalled the other evening to me. She turned to me. "I beg your pardon," she said, "but you are looking at us so oddly. Almost as if we were lunatics, right?"

I sighed a reproach. "I?"

But her glance and her smile were so enchanting I immediately ceased being angry. True, I felt like a sacrificial goat, but I deprecated this to myself. "I am not as naive as I appear," I thought.

Richie slid noiselessly across the terrace. I was beginning to dislike the lad. He had to shove in his two cents worth everywhere.

"He broke all the china yesterday," Eva remarked.

I had previously noticed that the service on the table was chipped and assembled from two sets; the teapot had no spout.

"How did it happen?" I inquired, casually.

"The usual way. He fell flat on his face. I found him lying on the rug with his face in the broken cups and saucers."

In my pocket I had a letter from my father and I decided to read it immediately. I excused myself and sat down at the other end of the terrace. Shortly afterwards I was left alone with Vavrzecki while Tykiewicz and his wife had gone along to pack his things. He was leaving for two weeks.

I wished to read my letter as quickly as possible as I suspected that my father was answering a certain question of mine. As I opened the envelope Vavrzecki suddenly asked me if I had any intention of marrying.

"Not at the moment," I answered, astonished. "Why do you ask?"

He remarked that marriage had many advantageous aspects and that in America marriages occurred at eighteen. "But this means nothing," he shrugged his shoulders and picked up the newspaper. I returned to my letter. After reading two sentences I was so overwhelmed by the contents that I missed falling over the balustrade by a hairsbreadth. My father had written:

> You ask about the Tykiewiczes but by now you surely know them better than I do. I know that Thomas Tykiewicz's life with his wife is an unhappy one. He had already tried to get a divorce three years ago but she refused to give it to him under any circumstances. They are a sad example of a mismated couple. Apparently under the guise of virtue and with the passing years his wife is torturing him horribly, although I have never heard him complain. He has a tender heart and a mild temper which make it difficult for him to leave her. Finally, I don't guarantee that this is not all gossip. . . ."

"Of course, it's gossip!" I cried out indignantly, "or else the old man has twisted things." I quieted when I caught Vavrzecki's heavy, unwinking gaze upon me.

"What's wrong with you?" he asked with cool interest. I detested him at that moment; I don't know why. All in all I felt a sudden dislike for the whole household living at the Black Slates. "What an unpleasant company!" I thought with aversion. "Beginning with you and ending with the servant-boy everyone acts like a lunatic!" Only the image of Eva retained its spotless purity in my imagination. "How could anyone conceive a thing like that!" my soul cried. "Such a creature certainly couldn't be capable of torturing anyone."

I went home, sat down on the porch and could not rid myself of my perturbation for a long time. At the very end of his letter my father had added, in a postscript, that he did not know Eva personally but had heard that she was very unsympathetic. "Unsympathetic," I mumbled under my breath. "Unsympathetic? It isn't fair to say a person is unsympathetic unless one knows him personally." Meanwhile, I watched the terrace of the Black Slates and saw Tykiewicz come out with his valise in hand, followed by his wife, cheerful, meek, smiling—like a beautiful, kind doll.

VII

Tykiewicz was to be gone for two weeks but he did not return for more than two months. Of course, during this time his doubtful domestic felicity was definitely destroyed. The relations grew more tense until at last there came a resolution on a memorable August evening. I recall that evening when crime hung over the villa of the Black Slates with heavy distaste. Tykiewicz appears to me to be a mysterious and sad figure as also does his presumably helpless and indifferent friend. I am ready to swear that the conduct of both was not unpremeditated and that the course of events unfolded according to a plan precisely devised by them. In any case, I am convinced that of them all Richie was the least culpable and if I did not fear that it would sound ridiculous I would consider his conduct as almost noble. After the events, when I visited him in the corrective institution he appeared to me normal and accountable for his actions; moreover, I am convinced that he only pretended to be repentant but in his soul felt doubtful and was certain of his correctness rather than of misgivings. It is characteristic that Tykiewicz then began to consider him as an irresponsible psychopath, he, who two months previously had defended Richie against me with such fury in his eyes. Be it as it may, the night of which I am speaking could have become something constructive rather than destructive in the life of the boy, as long as it did not awaken criminal instincts in him. When he saw me in the institution he was as naively happy as a child.

"I knew you would come," he said, "because, of course, we are partners."

I let that go in one ear and out the other since I could not endure having him believe us to be co-conspirators.

"Do they treat you well here?" I asked.

"They make me work very hard," he complained darkly. "I'm afraid my strength won't last. Even in my sleep I can't rest."

"In your sleep?"

"Yes. Because I'm always dreaming of that night. Why didn't you come and help me then?" he concluded. "After all, I know you understood everything just as I did. Why didn't you stop me?"

"I was too late," I answered. "By the time I got off the

porch and oriented myself to what was going on it was already too late."

He gave me a doubtful glance. He always suspected me of something.

"I don't know," he said, "perhaps you tricked me, like Tykiewicz."

This was what I was concerned about. I therefore asked him hurriedly if he still believed that Tykiewicz had tricked him. Yes. He was steadfastly certain but could not figure out how it had happened. Again he glanced at me, seeking support and confirmation, and, not finding it, suddenly doubted himself. He began to mumble under his breath as if he were humming. At last he cried, "Then why did he come to me that night?"

To me also this fact appeared to weigh greatly against Tykiewicz. In my bones I felt that his coming to the kitchen at one in the morning was certainly not for a drink of water, as he stated later. It must be understood that this was the most obscure point in the case. Richie was of the same opinion.

"After all, I did set out a carafe of water for him, as usual. He couldn't have drunk it. He must have poured it into the pail for the pail was full of clean water." He declared that he remembered this vividly.

The next thing which intrigued me was whether Tykiewicz was really drunk that night or pretending to be. When he came to the kitchen he was completely sober. In fifteen minutes, when all this happened and I ran into their corridor out of breath, I detected a heavy stench in the house and the smelly odor of alcohol on Tykiewicz's lips. This wasn't strange for lately he and his friend had been drinking heavily, but what is important, it is clear, is that that evening Tykiewicz did not drink at all. I am personally certain that he was able to dissimulate brilliantly. Only once do I remember catching him in an imprudence.

This was a few days after his arrival. He left his house, ostensibly going for a walk, but I have a feeling that he wanted to see me. He walked down the path, flourishing his hands amusingly and continually leaning leftward as if fighting the wind. Only when he sat down beside me did I realize he was drunk. I concealed my disgust with difficulty.

"Don't look at me that way, Edward, don't. We'll drink more tonight."

"I'm not allowed to drink," I said.

"Ah, foolishness." He began to mumble and suddenly dropped his head nearly to the ground. I thought he was about to fall and grasped him by the arm, but at that moment he cried, "Look, Edward!" I too bent down and saw the thing at which he was looking. It was an ant pushing a fairly large horsefly backwards, forcing it to march in the direction chosen by the ant. The horsefly, helpless and clumsy, occasionally tried to deviate from the path but the ant pushed it harder, or circled it until the fly again began to creep in the direction the ant had chosen.

"Look, Edward, doesn't this remind you of something?" the engineer cried and suddenly chuckled with a giddy, drunken laugh. He wiped his moist, bald head and abruptly asked enigmatically, "Would you like to be that fly?" He laughed until my flesh crept. Then, choking on his own laughter, he patted me on the shoulder. "Calm yourself," he said. "I have another bug—not you."

There was a reference hidden in these words whose meaning I understand only now. But meanwhile, depending on my naivety, he could permit himself this indiscretion. The next day he came round to apologize.

"I talked nonsense last night," he said. "Strictly speaking, I don't even know what I was babbling about. Ah, Edward, if you only knew how weary I am." At his departure he asked whether or not he had made any reference to a lady. "No? Really? Come see us this evening," he urged.

However, I did not go as I was avoiding visiting them. It was especially saddening to me to see Eva, who had become unrecognizable during the past two months. She had become not only inhospitable but almost distant in her attitude toward me. She tried to push me away as far as possible so that I would not be a witness to her manner of living and womanly joy, although it was transparently clear that she was happy. During her husband's absence I always saw her with Vavrzecki, radiant and enamored. Deep in my soul I felt resentment toward her but in the end I always justified her for one reason or another. During this time her power over me was great and unhealthy; I was able to look upon all her actions, good or evil, with equal delight. Moreover, in spite of everything, I did not believe that she was really betraying her husband. I preferred to believe that I suffered hallucinations rather than attribute the true meaning to the facts. Shortly afterwards, however, I was forced to believe that Eva was untrue to her husband and was living with his friend Vavrzecki. This was a great blow to me.

Once, when I was bustling around my house, Richie

sprang out from behind a bush. His eyes were red and puffed. He began to tell me that he wanted to leave the Tykiewiczes and that not for anything would he remain in their employ any longer. Then he asked whether I knew why Tykiewicz had not returned. I had no chance to answer as something occurred which attracted our attention. Raised voices sounded through the villa of the Black Slates and someone called out, "Really, you're terrible!" We saw a packet of paper fly out the open window of Vavrzecki's room. The wind snatched the sheets immediately and carried them in all directions. "Go pick them up!" I cried to Richie. The boy did not move from his tracks. Someone pushed aside the curtain in the window and we saw a part of Vavrzecki's room—a couch on which Eva was sitting and a large table covered with papers with Vavrzecki bent over it. We also saw Eva rise quickly, run to the table, snatch a heap of papers, and again a whole packet of sheets flew through the window. I thought I was dreaming. "Have they gone mad or something?" But I immediately turned my back on the window since it was an unpleasant experience for me to watch the manner in which Eva and Vavrzecki kissed. Only her movements impinge on my memory; they were almost rapacious as she threw herself on Vavrzecki, grasping his head with both hands as if it was a jug of water or wine. The curtain dropped. "Pick up the sheets!" I cried to Richie, who stood with staring eyes. "What are you gawking at?" He began gathering them up unwillingly. One of the sheets came to my hand by accident. It was a photograph of some kind of pier. The rest of the papers were also plans, photographs, and diagrams. I recalled Eva's antipathy toward her husband's profession. As she had once disliked electrical works did she now dislike bridges and viaducts? After Richie had gathered up the papers I carried them myself to Vavrzecki's window. I could not restrain myself from this show of spitefulness.

"Hello," I said. "I've found a pile of some kind of plans. I don't know how they got here." Inside the room the conversation was fairly quiet. Eva's voice reached me, "I was already sure that you were to be mine when you wanted to hit me in the corridor." Vavrzecki answered with conscious effort. "I did not suspect then that anything of the sort could happen. This is a wicked thing to do to Thomas."

"My dear, how funny you are. After all, Thomas and I have not loved each other for a long time."

"You're just talking—I know that he loves you."

"Hello!" I shouted. "I've found some kind of plans out here!" Silence followed. The curtain moved; I thought that I would now see Vavrzecki, but it was Eva who looked out the window. She smiled serenely. I admired her composure, bordering on shamelessness.

"Thank you," she said, "the wind caught them. There was a terrible draft in the room."

My rage took immediate flight and I again yielded to this woman's charm. "I must get away from here," I thought, when I found myself at home. It was raining. A storm raged over my hut. "As long as I stay here I'll be involuntarily meddling in their lives which, of course, I have no right to do. Why should I upset myself? I must leave!" And I wanted to pack my things immediately but suddenly I remembered that Richie too wanted to leave the Tykiewiczes and this foolish coincidence dissuaded me from departing. Anyway, it is probable that I would not have gone anywhere, since it was predestined that I pursue the development of the events whose concrete and tragic denouement came on that August night.

VIII

I will admit that I never had the courage to ask Tykiewicz bluntly if he really found himself in the kitchen accidentally and if there had been no water in his carafe in the bedroom. I had to be satisfied with his assertion in the corridor that he had come to the kitchen feeling a great thirst, and that he stood at the sink at the time when Richie sat in the window staring at the moon like a sleepwalker.

"I didn't notice anything peculiar about the lad," he said. "I know, of course, that he is odd and, anyway, there was no reason why he shouldn't watch the moon as long as he wanted." But more than this he would not say, how he met Vavrzecki for the last time before the accident, and what the reason was for their not meeting later in the corridor. I recall that already that night I could not understand that tragic *quid pro quo*. After all, two men just couldn't wander through a six-room house without meeting. But to get back to Tykiewicz, I judge that he was not quite so drunk as to utter all sorts of nonsense to Richie while in the kitchen and not remember any of it. Obviously it would be simple to allay all suspicion the moment we begin considering the boy as abnormal and to place all the blame on him.

Tykiewicz profited quickly from this when he declared on the spot, "You were right, Edward! Why didn't I immediately throw out this idiot and scoundrel?" As he said this he was so overcome that he braced himself against the corridor wall to avoid falling. Then, with a strange stubbornness he underlined that he had been drunk besides. This was really possible as he got drunk very quickly. He was not accustomed to alcohol. I knew that he was abstemious by inclination, and apparently he had not drunk a drop from the day of his marriage. He usually said he was indebted to his wife for this. For that reason I was quite surprised when he brought back several bottles of cognac on his return home in the middle of August.

His return was truly significant. In the first place, it occurred unexpectedly at an unusual hour. He had written that he was returning Monday morning; however, he arrived, and on foot, late on Saturday evening. I was the first to know this.

I awaited his arrival with growing uneasiness. The mode of life at the villa of the Black Slates appeared too drastic and provoking to me for there to be no catastrophe resulting from it. Vavrzecki and Eva would not part for even a moment. Whole days I observed them in uninhibited positions and sickeningly affectionate on the terrace.

Now they came out to breakfast together but not at eight in the morning as the two men had done, but at eleven, or even at noon. I was no longer interested in them. I came to the conclusion that my father had been right about this ending in a divorce court after which Vavrzecki would marry Eva. The only thing I didn't know was what Tykiewicz's attitude was toward his wife and if he had actually ceased to love her. In any case, it appeared that way. Such was my reasoning. But my intuition suggested another conclusion. Therefore, I was frightened when, in the evening, I saw a lantern on the high road leading from town and understood its significance.

It looked just like a glow-worm. At first I looked blankly at the little light shimmering in the distance, then as it began to grow larger and come closer, I knew it was a flashlight in the hands of some passerby. "Surely Tykiewicz must be returning, but why on foot?" I thought, and even though this could just as well have been someone else, some other vacationer, I was oddly certain that it was really Tykiewicz. "Oh, this is terrible!" I cried and looked out the window. The lights were already out in the Tykiewiczes' house; the flashlight was but fifty yards away.

"This doesn't concern me!" I consoled myself, but in my soul I felt fear. It grew when I saw the person with the flashlight pass the Tykiewiczes' house and rather than going in enter my footpath instead. "In that case it isn't Tykiewicz!"

But it was. He clambered heavily on the porch with a small valise in one hand and the flashlight in the other.

"How nice that you're not yet asleep, Edward. I've given you all a surprise, eh?" He removed his hat and wiped his bald head with a handkerchief.

"I've pleased you, haven't I? I came on foot because I wanted to take a walk. I left my things at the station. I saw your light and dropped in. And now, you know, I'm afraid to go home and wake Eva; she might be frightened, don't you think?" He grasped me by the arm and shook it—fat, sorrowing, childish. As usual he aroused a certain loving pity toward himself. "In fact, I dropped in on you so that you could wake them while I hid somewhere. That will be a surprise, won't it? What's new? I hope nothing has happened."

I could not look into his eyes and I didn't know what to say. He went on, excited and disagreeably gay. "What a joke! By God, but I've brought a valuable cargo with me, haven't I? Look!" He opened the valise and with astonishment I saw a dozen bottles of brandy. "I dragged this along the road and thought I'd die, it's so heavy. I had to leave one bottle by the roadside, but don't worry, it was empty."

"I thought you didn't drink," I interrupted.

"You're wrong, Edward, you're wrong. I always drank. Is there anything wrong with that? Well then, let us go, Edward. Lead the way. And sing, so that they will be properly surprised."

Forcibly he pushed me from the room and dragged me after him in the direction of the villa. Suddenly he began to roar at the top of his voice. He sang like a drunken cab driver, but it seemed to me he was play acting and that he was not truly drunk and happy.

"We'll sing together, right? The Marseillaise." And faking, in a hoarse voice, he sang, *Aux armes, citoyens!*

"Bang on the window, Edward, bang without mercy. Ah see, Jan has already awakened."

And in fact, Vavrzecki's bedroom light went on. Tykiewicz's eagerness apparently took flight. Flabbily, he leaned on my arm and we waited on the terrace steps. Shortly, Vavrzecki emerged; he was in pajamas and he wore a hair net on his head. Tykiewicz aimed a ray of light at him but immediately snapped off the flashlight.

"I have returned," he said. I saw his pale figure move closer to Vavrzecki and I heard them embrace.

"I returned earlier because I wanted to surprise you. Perhaps I shouldn't wake Eva?" Without bidding me good-night he disappeared into the house.

When I recall this scene now it appears to be a horrid comedy. But at that time I was too naive to grasp its delicate undercurrents. I was only impressed by the repellent sight of the drunken Tykiewicz which awakened a tender-hearted sympathy. "Why did he bring so much alcohol with him? Now he will drink himself to death." This was my belief and therefore I merely nodded my head sadly the next day when I saw a bottle on Tykiewicz's table. From now on he would never be without one.

Already at eight in the morning I heard the clink of glasses and Tykiewicz's hoarse, drunken voice as the engineers breakfasted in their pajamas. Instead of strawberries there were sharp cheeses on the table—the villa had changed to an unhealthy, smelly tavern. Apparently Vavrzecki drank less; in any case, it was not noticeable that he was drunk. On the other hand, Tykiewicz soaked up cognac from morning to night. They became very talkative. I could hear their excited, argumentative voices; they seemed to be quarreling about something without pause. Eva again disappeared and emerged on the terrace only in the afternoon, when the heat lessened. Outwardly it appeared that the men paid not the slightest attention to her.

I now visited them rarely. Once, when I did come, I met only Tykiewicz. He sat in a chair holding a glass of brandy and soda and with a troubled expression observed the amber fluid. His suit was spotty and dirty, his cheeks poorly shaven.

"What a terrible heat wave," he panted. "Care for a drink, Edward?"

I refused firmly and then asked warily, "Why do you drink so much?"

"Drink?" he repeated distractedly. "See, Edward, friendship is a wonderful thing! I am very happy that you believe in friendship!" He closed his eyes and I would have been certain that he had fallen asleep were it not that he continued, in a sleepy voice, "When two people become friends they create a strength greater than an army's. . . ."

I did not know that this noble thought could conceal an ordinary villainy.

"Oh yes, you are right," I said with pathos.

He stirred from his alcoholic nap and again looked at the glass. "Except, Edward, it's too bad that the notion of good is relative. Don't protest, Edward. Sometimes harming oneself is a greater wrong than harming another. I tell you, sometimes it is a sin to wrong oneself because it is a crime."

"I don't know what you mean," I began but he suddenly shuddered and his shout pierced the house, "Aaah!"

His bald head became violet. "Ah?" he inquired once more. "I thought you were saying something? I didn't quite hear you, did I? About friendship. Yes, yes. . . ."

He babbled whatever came to his tongue. He did not even cut short his babbling when Eva and Vavrzecki came out. She greeted me mechanically and said, "Oh, you look fine. You'll see, the climate in the hills will revive you completely."

She looked at me as though I were an empty space. I had the feeling that I was not even on the terrace. I was still a *quantité négligeable* to her, but to this my soul was resigned.

IX

At the corrective institution Richie told me that on that August night, when the disaster occurred, he had not slept at all as Tykiewicz had chivvied him all day long.

"I was frightened," he said. "From morning to night he kept button-holing me in the corridor, the kitchen, and the backyard, and continually saying something to me."

He said that as a result of these persecutions and, one could say, moral pressure, he became totally confused. This was the reason why, when Tykiewicz came during the night—allegedly for a glass of water—Richie became so frightened.

"I jumped off the window and my teeth began to chatter," he said. Tykiewicz never mentioned that. On the contrary, Tykiewicz said that he should have had reason to be frightened had he not been acquainted with Richie's eccentricities. "Why, he even tried to knock the glass of water out of my hand! I cursed him, 'What's the matter with you, fool?'" Really, it was difficult to determine who was telling the truth about that incident. I am inclined to think that the truth is somewhere in between; that it is in a strange key and for that reason so incomprehensible. Note, that in spite of the complete faith I had in Richie after these events, I refer to his testimony with great reservations. His psychology was ambiguous; the case itself, I will admit, was two-sided, and Richie was not certain which of these sides was the true one. Anyway, he could never discover it, everything was so completely tangled. On the one hand, he felt that he was influenced by personal motives and would beat his breast in sorrow, considering himself a criminal. On the other hand, he accounted for it by believing that Tykiewicz had forced him into it in some mysterious manner and then he would curse Tykiewicz, satisfied that he could lay the blame on another. But in either case it was evident that he acted in a state of beclouded intelligence, a somnambulistic trance; to a certain extent this could justify his actions.

"Then why did he come to me for a glass of water?" he cried to me in despair. I could give him no answer to that. "I know he was swallowing that water with distaste, that's how thirsty he was!"

"You're spouting foolishness," I said severely, but without conviction. "For just a remark like that you deserve to be put in jail."

He began to cry and mumble that I must be right and that he was besmirching an innocent man in order to escape responsibility. He accused himself of ingratitude and betrayal of the master who had raised him and been his protector.

"How's that?" and only then did I learn that Tykiewicz had taken him from home as a small child and trained him to be a footman.

"He was always very good to me and spoke so kindly that I wanted to cry. Especially that last day. . . ."

"What last day was that?" I asked. I was able more or less to reconstruct his action on the basis of his quite incoherent confessions. I was most irritated that Richie felt he had a complaint against me in that I had not aided

him and did not support him in his aim to leave the Tykiewiczes. That day, when Tykiewicz caught him in the
yard, Richie declared positively that he wanted to leave
his service and return to his family in the village.

"You'll go nowhere," the engineer was supposed to have
retorted. "Are you badly treated here?"

Richie was sullenly silent. Tykiewicz began to tell him
at length how he was prized and liked by Eva. "Aren't
you ashamed to be leaving your lady?" he said. Richie
squirmed, rooted to the spot. Within his soul everything
was confused. Tykiewicz, already quite drunk, kept stam-
mering something about loyalty and love with such ani-
mation and strength that his cheeks puffed out. It seemed
he was blowing out a hidden flame inside Richie. The
boy completely lost his usual indifference. He fell under
the influence of the engineer's speech to such an extent
that he escaped to the cellar and spent two hours there
without showing his nose. He emerged only because Eva
began to play the piano and the sounds lured him out.
His love of hearing her play was morbid.

After a two-month break—during that time she hadn't
touched the keys even once—and not until the day of the
events about which I speak, did she remember her music.
She played through the whole afternoon. Chords and ca-
denzas cascaded through the windows and echoed in my
house, wild and alarming. I remember that I too was irritated by this unusually sensual music. It had a decidedly
depressing effect on Richie. He reacted toward it like a
dog. He almost whined with melancholy. When he
crawled out of the cellar he was paler than usual and
reeled through the house like a ghost at a seance. Tykiewicz again caught him in the corridor. "Do you hear how

beautiful the music is?" he said and clucked his tongue. Richie could not understand what the engineer wanted of him. He was saddened and frightened. The engineer trailed him everywhere. Unceasingly, he poured into Richie's head the idea that there was an evil spirit on earth and that this spirit had possessed their home and was ruining everything. "Our luck is gone; our luck is gone," he repeated. "Everything is spoiled. And you know who is doing this." There was no question but that Tykiewicz was well soused; one could have thought that he was on the verge of delirium tremens. But on the other hand this conjecture would belie the fact that he was so careful and deliberate that Vavrzecki's name did not even once fall from his lips. This would indicate a great internal mastery and calculation. He was able to entangle the boy without wholly showing his cards. Nothing strange, then, that Richie's dislike of those around him grew to a bursting abhorrence of all within a single day. He came running to me that day, seeking help, but unfortunately I did not understand a word of his hysterical utterances and threw him out the door. He stood before the porch and tugged his red tie. He was disheveled and his hands trembled. At last I became sorry for him. "Richie—," I began. But he was already running in the direction of the house.

X

It was clear whom Richie had in mind when he conceived his mad resolution, but it is not clear whom Tykiewicz was thinking of. It is difficult to know whether he had primarily planned this tragic *quid pro quo* as a scheme for an improbable game of hide-and-seek with Vavrzecki, or whether he had his own wife in mind. When he knocked on Vavrzecki's door that night Tykiewicz heard Jan's voice, which could not have made him uneasy in any way.

"Anyhow, nothing of the sort would have even come to my mind," he said. "All I heard was that Vavrzecki would not come to my room even though he was not asleep. He did not say that he would come right out. If that had been the case I would have waited for him! Instead, he said very clearly that he wanted Richie for something."

If Tykiewicz had been concerned about Vavrzecki he could have arranged this much more simply, since I am convinced that both would have come to an understanding, finally, on the basis of old friendship. It would have been more difficult to reach an understanding with Eva. However, as far as I could discern, Vavrzecki was more inclined to agree. When they quarreled it was evidently over trifles. Their spats rather had the character of courteous, friendly reciprocity. And if indeed Tykiewicz suggested to Vavrzecki, as was later said, that he would divorce his wife if Vavrzecki married her, then both were on the road to complete adjustment of their desires. Later it became clear that Vavrzecki did not agree to this. Meanwhile, a very ostentatious and noisy quarrel exploded between them. They shouted so loudly that passers-by stopped on the road and looked with alarm at the villa under the Black Slates. After the quarrel Vavrzecki and Eva went for a walk. Tykiewicz remained on the terrace and napped near his siphon. He did not even glance after them; one would have thought that he was totally unconcerned about them. Truly, Richie was more moved by their disappearance than Tykiewicz. The boy wandered dejectedly around the villa; he even searched the bushes as if they could hide there. For really, their going for a walk strongly resembled an escape. Like furtive thieves they went past my house. Eva kept urging Vavrzecki as if she was anxious to be alone with him. They returned after two hours, completely pacified now, narcotically intoxicated by their own tenderness.

"You'll see—somehow this will right itself," she said as they stole past my windows. Vavrzecki nodded his head doubtfully. I noticed that he had become very wan in the last few days.

This was the day which preceded the events. It passed with relative quiet. I know that the evening went by in an almost idyllic atmosphere. It recalled former times. They had afternoon tea and dinner together. There was no alcohol. A calm, friendly, atmosphere reigned over the terrace. Tykiewicz napped after dinner and became quite sober. He discussed something with Eva and begged her pardon. He said he had definitely given up drinking. He was still a trifle mopish and therefore retired to his room for a few hours with a compress for his head and read a book. Eva, as related, played the piano all afternoon and was in fine humor; no evil premonitions bothered her. Vavrzecki was also well disposed and worked that day, for the first time after a long interval. He remained in his room from tea-time until dinner, and even after dinner he could be seen hunched over the high drawing board.

Vavrzecki's bedroom was located far from the kitchen, at the other end of the corridor, across from Eva's bedroom.

Tykiewicz's study was a few doors further away. Richie and the old cook lived in the basement. But this evening Richie did not even go downstairs, he was so upset. He served at table during supper, mumbling under his breath a bit louder than usual, although the sight of pleasantly conversing people could not apparently excite suspicion. Looking at them, even I was led into error. I did not at all want to believe that I had been a witness to so many strange and unpleasant scenes. Had I dreamed all this or what, I thought. I judged that the domestic drama had been resolved in a manner unknown to me and that now there was nothing to be afraid of. Unfortunately, it was not that way. The night brought a most unexpected and sad conclusion.

XI

Coming to the description of this night I emphasize that I describe it on the basis of the accounts of all who witnessed it; I saw little myself. I arrived at the house of the Black Slates a good few minutes after the event. However, at that time I was already sufficiently oriented so that I eagerly committed every movement and every word to my memory.

What I saw could be summarized as follows.

Around midnight I extinguished my light. It was the night of the full moon and the wind blew occasionally. It bathed my room in a cool, unemotional light, and finally hung suspended over my window; its rays were so dazzling that it prevented my falling asleep. For a long time I turned from side to side, then, impatient, I determined to shade the window. The curtains were in the wash so I had to substitute a sheet for them. I climbed on the sill to locate a nail but was so overcome by the beauty of the night and the surrounding scenery that I paused motionless on the sill and looked around. The distant hills shone with silver; clear, phosphorescent clouds rushed across the sky. From time to time a breeze came along but the quiet rustle of the bushes and grass only emphasized the stillness.

Evidently everyone was asleep in the Tykiewiczes' house. After a time, however, I became sure that this was not so. To my amazement the kitchen door opened. Because no one came out for some time I thought a draft had opened it. The door was an opening through which I could observe the dark interior of the kitchen. "I hope no one robs them," I thought, but at that moment the door closed again. Now I was certain it was a draft. It astonished me only that it had opened and closed soundlessly. Then for a second time it opened, but now it was with a wild vehemence and Richie rushed out of the kitchen as if he had been propelled by a kick. I cursed myself, "Some kind of folly is beginning," and I was right. Richie's actions awakened my worst fears. Lowering his head and with stealthy tread he traversed the length of the house until at last he came to Vavrzecki's window. He paused, as if listening. "What's he doing there?" I thought, intrigued. "Is he a house burglar by any chance?" Just then Richie stretched out his hand with a cautious movement and touched the window. He was evidently checking it to see if it was locked. At that moment I decided to act. "I'll teach you a lesson!" I thought and I was about to run out on the porch in order to catch the boy red-handed.

Meanwhile Richie had found the window locked. For a moment he hung on the sill with his bare feet sticking out in the air, then he jumped down and disappeared in the direction of the terrace, growling and mumbling, as if possessed by the devil. He entered the terrace, taking it three steps at a time in an awkward but at the same time oddly lively manner, ran to the door, which was open, and disappeared into its maw.

I quickly threw on my clothes, and torn by all kinds of conjectures, went out. It was perfectly still. The light of the moon poured down so brightly that I could distinguish each blade of grass. I felt that my pulse had increased and that my nerves were strained to their utmost limits. Strictly speaking, I should immediately have gone to see what was happening in the Tykiewiczes' house. Senselessly I procrastinated, not realizing that every moment was an unpardonable delay. When at last I decided to go downstairs it was already too late. A strange sound dispersed through the villa under the Black Slates, like a mournful note ringing monotonously and without pause in the quiet night. I know that I had never heard such a sound—it was like nothing I had ever heard before— it was entirely different from any other sound. I jumped down the stairs and ran in the direction of this unearthly, monotonous cry, guided by instinct rather than reason. I passed bushes which disappeared before my eyes as if passed by a speeding automobile. Breathless, I ran onto the terrace and, like a bomb, went through the door into the corridor.

There was a bluish haze in the corridor. The cry, or rather, the monotonous wail, had not stopped. Here, before my eyes, I saw Tykiewicz's checkered figure and bald head.

"Who's that?" he shouted and grabbed me by the sleeve. "Edward, what's happened to Vavrzecki?" For a while we could not locate the doorknob, searching for it on the right when it was on the left. During this time the cry was cut short; we heard only a throaty rattle. We scuffled around the door, for now, instead of pushing it forward, Tykiewicz pulled it toward himself. "It's locked," he stammered. "It's locked!"

"Don't pull on it!" I shouted and caused him to release it with my fist. Then I drew him after me into Vavrzecki's room.

The light of the moon was reflected in a narrow, vertical stripe on the right wall. The rest of the room was in darkness. I saw the white bed and someone lying in it. A second person stood at the bedside. We immediately recognized Eva as the one lying in Vavrzecki's bed. She was sprawled in the depths of the pillows suggesting an attempt to conceal herself in their downiness and looked at us with a glassy, half-conscious gaze.

XII

A few minutes later, when Tykiewicz and I had departed to return to the corridor, he related the following.

"I was very thirsty, Edward," he said, "and because of that I could not fall asleep. As luck would have it there wasn't a drop of water in the carafe; Richie had evidently forgotten to fill it. Besides, I was horribly lonely and I felt with sorrow that I could not go on without some artificial stimulant." As if by design Tykiewicz here thrust his face closer to mine so that I got a whiff of wine. "The feeling of loneliness so depressed me that I would even have preferred the company of the devil rather than be all alone. It was already one in the morning by my watch and I knew that Eva was asleep by now, and since she had complained of being ill that morning I did not wish to disturb her. I decided to have a chat with Jan, if he was not yet asleep. I thought of this as I was going to the kitchen for a glass of water. I turned back when I was halfway there and knocked on Vavrzecki's door. It was quiet; I decided then that he had already fallen asleep. Then I heard his voice, 'What's wrong?' he asked. I suggested that he should come to my room, if he felt like it. 'Not for anything,' he said. 'Why are you wandering around at night!' Then he asked me to send Richie to him. 'Richie!' I said, dumbfounded. 'Yes, yes,' he answered. I swear on my word of honor, Edward, that's how it really was. Eh? You're surprised that he wanted Richie at that time of night, are you?"

I remember that Tykiewicz leaned on my arm giving an appearance of being drunk or deathly exhausted. I saw the shining baldness extending to his neck—I guess he had rested his head on his chest.

"So was I surprised," he said. "But Edward, you know I had a little under my belt, eh? 'Very well,' I agreed. 'I'll call Richie for you,' and I went to the kitchen. In the kitchen, though, Richie was sitting near the window, staring at the moon. 'What a fool you are,' I said to him, 'Why don't you go to bed?' But why should this concern me? He could stare at the moon all he wanted.

" 'Well, since you're still up, that's fine. Go to Mr. Vavrzecki—he's been calling you.' I drank some water and returned to my room. Before I had time to lie down I heard Vavrzecki's footsteps. I thought he had evidently gotten up and I went out to find him. I looked through the entire house and even heard him as he called, 'Thomas! Thomas!' and imagine it—to no avail. Then this happened and you came running, right? I never suspected that anything like this, anything like this. . . ."

He nearly sobbed; he attempted to take a few steps but failed and grasped at the wall. In spite of this his condition now did not, somehow, awaken any sympathy.

"Edward! Edward!" he cried, and his bald head twinkled before my eyes. "You were right about Richie, weren't you? He was sitting there, staring at the moon. 'Go at once,' I said, 'because Mr. Vavrzecki is calling!' I spoke a few more words to him which I can't recall now, out of weariness and too much drink. I did not even notice that he tried to knock the glass out of my hand!"

Richie gave me a slightly different version of this scene. It seems that in the Tykiewiczes' house no one but the cook slept that night. Richie did not even undress. He was afraid of the moon. I do not doubt that he suffered somewhat from lunacy. Therefore he sat at the window and everything was in turmoil inside him—at least that was the way he described his condition. He kept remembering Tykiewicz's persecutions and for some unknown reason felt terribly sorry for him. He had his own vague and strange thoughts and a morbid chaos of pictures in his brain. They unfolded before his eyes: Eva playing the piano, Vavrzecki going for a walk with her. The figure of Vavrzecki occasionally appeared to him as totally black, engulfed in ink from head to foot. Then again, all kinds of thoughts and sensations came to his head and, as he asserted, he didn't know whether they were his own or whether Tykiewicz had put them there. "It's true, there's an evil spirit in the house," he thought with superstitious fear. The silence, being alone, and the moon frightened him more and more until he was covered with gooseflesh. Queer and repulsive creatures danced before his eyes. One was bald, another had Vavrzecki's yellow hair and stuck his tongue out at him. "The Devil!" he thought. Other monsters were naked with large, ugly, protruding women's breasts. He said they did indecent things until he blushed with shame. Suddenly Tykiewicz appeared right under his nose: he was also naked and had a bottle under his arm. "We'll go to hell with you!" he shouted at Richie, "because we won't have the strength to fight our black spirit!" Richie knew who this black one was. He even felt he was bewitched by him; he wanted to pray but the moon prevented him. It extended long, green hands toward him and tried to lure him out the kitchen window. "Our Father—" Richie began, and then heard footsteps in the corridor. He was horrified. When he saw Tykiewicz entering the kitchen his teeth began to chatter.

"Not asleep yet?" Tykiewicz asked. "Not sleeping yet, eh? I came for water," but he did not go to the sink at all, as he later declared; he stopped in the center of the kitchen and spoke of something to Richie.

"What do you want of me, master?" Richie stammered out. Tykiewicz growled, "Nothing," that he wanted "Nothing" of him. "But I felt that he did want something of me," Richie said.

"I came for water," Tykiewicz declared, and only then went to the tap. Richie was seized by such mad alarm that he completely lost control of himself. "You didn't come for water: you're not thirsty," he shouted, seeing that Tykiewicz forced himself to drink with distaste. The boy even tried to snatch the glass from his hand but Tykiewicz pushed him aside.

"Have you gone mad!" he said harshly. And then Richie saw the normal Tykiewicz before him, quiet and poised. He was as sober as a boot; he did not totter at all as he had before. But this was short lived; after a moment he again began to speak in riddles.

"Eva liked you very much," he said, "very much. You're a lovable boy, aren't you?" he stroked Richie's head and the boy squirmed. "Aha," the engineer then said, "I almost forgot. Mr. Vavrzecki is not asleep yet and has been calling you. You'll go, won't you?" Finally, losing patience (for Richie stood rooted in place) he whispered violently, "Go to Vavrzecki at once. Do you understand who Vavrzecki is or don't you?"

From the beginning Richie subconsciously objected to this order but Tykiewicz added suddenly, "I'll show you, you fool," and Richie yielded to this threat. He had the feeling that everything within him had gone haywire. The monsters again appeared before his eyes, one more repulsive than the next. Then half-unconscious with fear, he opened the door to the yard. At first, however, he did not have the strength or courage to cross the threshold. "Our Father—" he repeated giddily and again closed the door. Everything in the kitchen observed him with human eyes. The moon beckoned him with such force that at last

Richie could not resist and running blindly as if he were asleep he jumped out into the yard. Vavrzecki's window was closed, therefore he ran around to the front.

XIII

That night around midnight Eva came to Vavrzecki as usual. She was so sure of her husband and his magnanimity that she never suspected he could follow or spy on her. But to prevent any accident she locked her door after leaving, then approached the study and peeked through a crack. Tykiewicz lay in bed, face turned to the wall. She was sure he was asleep and she knew his sleep was heavy. Completely at ease then, she went to Vavrzecki. He was waiting for her and when she entered he extinguished the candle burning on the table. She could not make out his face in the dusk, which she knew, womanlike, down to its finest detail. Possibly, if the window had not been so carefully shaded and if it had not been so dark she could have discerned a change in it which might have warned her or alarmed her. She would not have guessed anything anyway; she was blinded by an emotion which depraved her and deprived her of strength. She was physically drowsy and somnolent and moved with great difficulty. It seemed to her that her knees were made of cotton batting. This was both irritating and pleasant. But from the first moment she felt that Vavrzecki was not the same as always. "Perhaps he was already upset by premonitions?" she said later. "At that time, unfortunately, I noticed it only in passing and did not attribute any

107

meaning to it. Who says women have intuition? They have none!"

Suddenly she noticed that Vavrzecki was listening attentively to something. But a half-hour passed before she thought to ask him what the matter was. He answered that it seemed to him that someone was walking in front of the door in the corridor. Eva sobered and sat on the edge of the bed.

"Only then did I understand how careless I had been," she admitted with despair. "For almost an hour I was unaware of anything going on around me. I was deaf."

For some time she had the sensation that she had just returned to life from unconsciousness. A half-hour before the whole house could have toppled but not a sound would have reached her notice.

They sat there together, suppressing the breath in their chests. But around them everything was silent.

"You imagined it," she whispered. And at the same time she heard footsteps. Someone *was* walking in the corridor. She recognized the sound of the footsteps immediately. "It's Thomas," she whispered. "What does he want?" The footsteps neared and finally stopped in front of the door. "I wonder if he was coming to see me; perhaps something unexpected has happened? It's a good thing I locked my room." She listened to see if her husband was going to knock on her bedroom door. Instead of that someone knocked heavily on Vavrzecki's door.

"God pity me," Eva moaned and felt Vavrzecki's palm over her lips.

"Quiet!" he said in her ear and pretended to be snoring.

A second knock came at the door. To Eva it seemed that now the rapping was powerful and impatient. It did not pause for a moment but went on in a continuous hammering and echoing. She was ready to jump off the bed, then realized it was her heart hammering and palpitating.

"Who's there?" Vavrzecki asked, in a theatrically sleepy voice.

"Only me," Tykiewicz answered from the other side of the door. He spoke very calmly, and this gave Eva temporary relief.

"What's happened? Why are you wandering about at night?" Vavrzecki asked in the same, faked, sleepy tone. He tore his hand away from Eva's lips as she suddenly bit his finger.

"It would be better if you didn't answer at all," she whispered. But he ignored her.

"What do you want?" he asked.

"Open up," Tykiewicz said from the corridor, and Eva threw herself backward so that she bumped against the railing of the bed. "Open up," Tykiewicz repeated, "or come see me. I can't get to sleep. If you feel up to it we can have a chat. How about it?"

Vavrzecki rose silently and put on his slippers.

"Very well. I'll come right away," he said quietly, almost coolly.

"Go to your room and I'll be there at once," he repeated. He took several quick steps and leaned with his back against the door. Of course he did not even mention Richie's name. Why should he have wanted him!

The corridor became silent. Then Tykiewicz's voice uttered a statement which seemed bereft of sense; "Good! I'm going to the kitchen anyhow."

The inconsistency of this statement was forcefully evi-

dent but Eva did not have time to think. When she heard
Tykiewicz's footsteps going in the direction of the kitchen
she felt joy and a relief from tension. She trembled from
head to foot; this was truly a fever of happiness. Vavrzecki
opened the door and looked out into the corridor.

"No one there," he said. "I'll go to him while you wait
a while before slipping out to your room."

She would not agree to that for anything.

"Don't go, don't go!" she begged. She agreed, however,
because there was no other way out.

Generally so confident of herself, now that all danger
had passed Eva, for some mysterious reason, lost her head.
She made many superfluous movements; she straightened
her hair, looked for the belt of her dressing gown, picked
up her slippers and placed them on top of the quilt. She
was then ready to jump out of the bed but again heard
chilling footsteps in the corridor and the door opened a
second time. But it opened very slowly.

XIV

Vavrzecki walked through the corridor, looked into
Tykiewicz's room, then the kitchen, but neither here nor
there did he find anyone. Then, hearing footsteps and a
rustle at the front door, he went to the parlor and at last
began to look for Tykiewicz through the whole house.
Apparently, he even began to call to him, "Thomas,
Thomas!" But he did not find him. In this way two men
hunted each other for several minutes, lost in a six-room
house. But really, everything might have been somewhat
different.

When she saw the door opening Eva immediately felt that a disaster had taken place and that now the end of everything would follow. That is why she immediately recognized her husband in the figure that slid into the chamber. "Thomas!" she wanted to whisper pleadingly, but the name did not emerge from her throat and she was only able to gasp out, "-massss!" She saw her husband take a few groping steps, hands outstretched before him, feeling the atmosphere; "-masss," she hissed once more and suddenly was seized by maddening, stabbing pains in her belly. She could move neither hand nor foot. She stared as in a fog at the shape of her husband which slowly neared the bed. At that a sharp, cold idea came to her rescue. "If I hide my head under the quilt," she thought, "my husband will think it is Vavrzecki sleeping here!" But instead of bringing succor, this idea brought ruin. Very quietly, with almost imperceptible movements she pulled the sheet over herself until she was totally hidden under it. Then she saw nothing except the light outline of her own dressing-gown collar. Cowering in the bed, she was helpless and impotent; her fear grew to monstrous size. She heard, or rather felt, her husband bend over her and stand motionless. Suddenly, a dreadful thought came into her head; it was a certainty that Tykiewicz was not looking at her now but at the slippers which she had placed beside her on the bed. She heard his uneven and wheezing breath practically in her ear. Again a great deal of time passed until at last she could no longer endure it and she decided at any cost to find out if her husband was really looking at the slippers. The cramps in her belly intensified. Twisting her lips with pain she began to slide the edge of the sheet off her right eye. She could no longer bear the uncertainty, she had to see, she would go insane. It seemed to her, as her husband stood bent over her, that an hour had already passed. When at last she uncovered her eye she saw someone else's eyes before her, staring eagerly into hers. They looked at each other in this manner for a few moments. The eyes were no more than a three-finger width away from her face; they seemed huge and heavy, like two black stones. Then, to her dreadful amazement Eva realized that it was not her husband standing over her but Richie.

This was even worse. "I thought I'd die," she told me later. "His face was so odd, so repulsive, that I suspected Lord knows what. I knew all the time, of course, that the boy was madly in love with me and, unfortunately, I even excited and teased his love. I realized that now he would throw himself upon me but I could not cry out because if I did Thomas would really come running!"

She continued to lie motionless and that same lovely, sirupy feeling of having all her joints made of cotton batting engulfed her afresh. She knew that she would now be unable even to struggle. Ineffectually, she tried to resist this drastic weakness of the flesh. But luckily the strength returned to her limbs in a while, when she realized that there was no sensual desire in Richie's eyes. There was murder in his eyes. She wanted to throw off the quilt—to hell with everything! But instead she cowered even more and again pulled the sheet over herself. At that moment she felt the pillow torn from beneath her head and thrown over her face. She tried to free herself and struggled on the mattress until her legs hung over the edge to the floor. She had nothing to breathe with now; she could not cry out and someone's hands choked and

gagged her more and more. At last she was able to free
her face and began to scream, to be heard through the
house, not recognizing her own voice. Then she saw that
Richie's eyes were assuming a different expression.

The eyeballs straightened, the whites disappeared—the
look became humble and sane. Slowly he released Eva's
throat and stood upright at the head of the bed.

"It isn't—" he began stammeringly, "it isn't Mr. Vavrzecki?"

At that instant Tykiewicz and I rushed into the room.

XV

The finding of one's wife in the bed of a friend is, of
course, sufficient grounds for divorce.

I met Eva the next day in the first-class waiting room
of the station. She carried a traveling bag and a blanket.
The expression on her face was one of sorrow but I did
not notice any embarrassment. She smiled like a doll.

"Ah, it's you," she said. "Evidently the mountains don't
agree with you since you're leaving."

I was near despair but at the moment I said nothing to
her. On the other hand she was unusually talkative.

"Do you know that a man and a woman look at good
in a completely different way?" she asked. "To a man
good lies in a woman's flesh; to a woman in his soul." I
was silent and embarrassed. "I feel that you are my
friend," she continued, and for the first time looked at me
carefully. "I say they are scoundrels!" I managed a protest. "Yes, scoundrels," she replied harshly. "Do you realize they both knew I was sleeping with each of them

at the same time. And in front of my eyes they pretended to believe in me. . . ."

Her cynicism appalled me.

"Perhaps it's unpleasant for you to talk about this," I interrupted.

"No. At least *you* should know everything. They shared me between them, when I. . . ." I thought she was about to say—when I loved only one—but evidently it was not proper for her to say this.

Suddenly she called out with passion. "How glad I am that at last I'm free! I don't want to look at a man. How dared he say that it was impossible to get rid of a woman; that even though she ceases to love a man, a woman will not give him his freedom for anything under the sun; that she is like a dog lying in a manger—can't eat it herself and won't permit anyone else to do so. It's a lie, for I was the first to ask for a divorce!" She broke off and prevailed over her tears with difficulty. Then she began to complain that it was all because of that foolish and horrible accident. She spoke with such charming shamelessness that I looked upon her with enchantment. I allowed her that opinion. Anyhow, who can be sure that it was really not that way.

"The Express," the porter called at the door of the platform.

"Where are you going?" she asked.

"Wherever you go," I answered with banal gallantry, at the same time feeling that something final and frightful would immediately happen. "I am your friend," I stammered.

"Ah, yes," she said slowly, and looked me over from head to foot, as if I were a dummy in a window display.

I said I had loved her for many, many months. She smiled, beautiful and doll-like, and nodded her head. Then, along with that nod, it seemed to me a door was closed. And when we kissed in the compartment she looked at me with curiosity.

"Of course, you won't believe the gossip that I terrorized my husband," she said.

BRUNO SCHULZ was shot by the Nazis in 1942. He was a teacher of drawing who surprised the Polish literary world with his collections of short stories: *Sklepy cynamonowe* (*The Cinnamon Shops*), published in 1934, and *Sanatorium pod klepsydrą* (*Sanatorium Under the Hourglass*), published in 1937. Schulz's world is a fantastic one in which reality is distorted sometimes in a frightening but always in an artistically convincing fashion. A collected edition of his works is now being prepared in Poland and should gain him the greater prominence he justly deserves.

W. STANLEY MOSS, with his wife, ZOFIA TARNOWSKA, translated the whole of *Sanatorium Under the Hourglass*. The following story was selected from its unpublished text. Moss is the author of a number of books, among them *The Hour of Flight, Ill Met by Moonlight* and *A War of Shadows*.

My Father Joins the Fire Brigade

BRUNO SCHULZ

*M*y mother and I had been for a holiday at a summer resort in the neighboring county—a delightful spot, situated in the wooded basin of the river Slotwinka, through which there filtered the fountains of a thousand little streams. It was during the first days of October that we returned, and in my ears there still echoed the rustling of the alder groves and the warbling of the birds. We made the journey in an old landau which had such a large hood that it looked exactly like a traveling road-house. We sat crushed beneath a mass of luggage in a deep, velvet-padded alcove, and we saw the scenery out of the window as though it were a series of picture-postcards of the landscape being slowly shuffled from hand to hand.

Towards evening we arrived upon a large, windswept plateau. The sky hovered above its crossroads in deep silence, the winds flitted across the colorful rosette. Here was the toll-gate between the two counties, and this was the last point before the landscape opened up into the vast lateness of autumn. At the boundary there stood a weather-beaten signpost. The inscriptions upon it had been obliterated, and it was being buffeted playfully by the wind.

The landau's wheel-rims grated to a standstill in the sand; its talkative, glittering spokes became silent; and only the massive hood, poised like Noah's Ark in a desert, continued to be rocked by the wind which swept across the road.

My mother paid the toll-fee. With a creaking of hinges the bar of the toll-gate was raised, and then the coach drove ponderously on into the autumn.

Our road took us across a large expanse of flat country. Here the scenery seemed to be pale and discolored, fading away into an insipid infinity; and, in the distance, the heaviness of a late storm was gathering.

As though one were turning over the yellowed pages of an old book, the leaves of the landscape became ever weaker and more wan. Without knowing it we might well have traveled through this windy nirvana beyond the realms of time and reality. We might have remained forever as a part of this sterile picture, imprisoned in our motionless coach among the clouds of the parchment sky —like an old illustration, a forgotten engraving, a crumbling manuscript—but suddenly, with a jerk of the reins, the coachman pulled us out of this lethargic scene and guided the landau into a forest.

We entered the tobacco-like atmosphere of a thick, withering dryness. Everything around us became cosily brown, like a box of coronas, and the tree-trunks which drifted past us in the semi-darkness were as brittle and as aromatic as cigars. The coachman had no matches and was unable to light the lanterns, so the horses were obliged to follow the road by instinct. As their pace slowed down the rattle of the spokes became quieter and the wheels drove softly through the scented carpet of the pine-needles. My mother fell asleep. I did not notice the time going by, and all I was conscious of was the roar of the forest which clamored above the hood of the coach. But finally the earth beneath the horses' hooves suddenly stiff-ened into the hard paving of a city street. The coach turned around and came to a standstill, stopping so close to the wall of our house that it must almost have grazed it. My mother alighted and groped for the front gate, and the coachman unloaded the baggage.

We entered the hall. Inside it was warm and dark and quiet, like an empty bakery early in the morning when the stoves have gone out. We could hear the sound of the crickets outside the windows as they patiently tried to unpick the stitches of light from the obscurity of the night. Fumbling along the wall, we found the staircase.

When we reached the creaky landing at the turn of the stairs, my mother said: "Wake up, Joseph. You're drop-ping off to sleep. Come along, there are only a few more steps." But I could keep awake no longer and, clutching her even closer to me, I fell soundly asleep.

Afterwards I was never able to find out from my mother exactly how much of what I saw that night was, in fact, reality, and how much of it was the fruit of my slumber-ing imagination.

A great debate was taking place between my father, my mother and Adela, the last-named of whom was the pro-tagonist of the scene; and, as I have now realized, this argument had a great fundamental significance. There are gaps in my memory about it all, and the blind stains of sleep are to be blamed for the amount of conjecture and hypothesis with which I have had to fill in the breaches. I remember how I floated along inertly, with the night-breeze fluttering upon my closed eyelids like washing on a clothes-line. The night had cast off its transparent veil of stars and from high above was peeping into my slumbers with its old, eternal face. The twinkle of a remote star, trapped between my eyelashes, spilled its silver over the blind whites of my eyes, and through the slits of my eyelids I could see the candle-lit room around me as though it had been caught in a confusion of golden sparks.

It is quite possible that this entire scene took place on a totally different occasion. Many things point to the possibility that I witnessed it at a much later date—on a day, in fact, after we had closed the shop, when I was returning home with my mother and the shop assistants.

On the threshold of the lobby my mother uttered a cry of mingled astonishment and rapture, while the assistants stood dumbfounded. In the middle of the room there stood a simply magnificent, brazen knight-at-arms, a genuine Saint George, arrayed with golden bucklers upon his armlets, a fine belt on his cuirass, and an entire outfit of clinking, burnished armor. It was with joy and admiration that I recognized my father's bristling beard and mustache sprouting out from beneath the heavy, praetorial helmet. The armor undulated with the heaving of his breast and, like the body of some enormous beetle, it breathed through the opening and closing of its polished brass rings. Magnified by his apparel and radiating the brightness of his golden plating, he looked exactly like the commander-in-chief of a heavenly host.

"Unfortunately, Adela," he was saying, "you have never been able to understand anything which is on a high level. However, now that I'm riveted into my armor I can scoff at that nagging nature of yours which used to drive me to despair. See how your impotent fury has left you tongue-tied. Your choice of words has been vulgar, loose and totally lacking in good taste. Believe me when I tell you that your display has filled me with only pity and sadness because, since you were born without any imagination, you burn with envy at the thought of anything which rises above the commonplace."

Adela looked my father up and down with an expression of illimitable contempt, and then, turning to my mother and shedding uncontrollable tears of irritation, she said: "He's pinching all our raspberry juice! He's taking every bottle of it from the house! Think of it, after all the trouble we've gone to in making it during the summer! He gives it to those good-for-nothing pumper pals of his. And, what's more, he showers me with rudeness." She gave a little sob. "Captain of the fire-brigade, indeed! Captain of a whole bunch of scoundrels!" She treated my father to a hateful look. "I'm fed up with them. They're all over the place. Every morning when I go to the bakery I can't open the door because there are two of them sleeping on the doorstep; and then, sound asleep in their brass helmets, they sprawl across every step on the staircase. When they wake up they go scrounging in the kitchen and poke their faces—rabbit-faces with brass tins on top—through the cracks in the door and whine like schoolboys for sugar. They dance around me, ogling, and all but wag their tails. They blink at me and lick their chops in a most disgusting manner. And those are the people who get our raspberry juice!"

"Your common nature," my father retorted, "defiles

everything that it touches. You have painted a picture of these sons of fire which is certainly worthy of your shallow mind. As for myself, my entire sympathy goes out to this unfortunate race of salamanders; my heart bleeds for their poor, disinherited beings. The only fault they ever committed was that they devoted themselves to the service of humanity. This magnificent race of men gave its services to the people for a spoonful of miserable food, and all it received in return was pure contempt. The obtuseness of the plebs is beyond words. Is it surprising that they don't like their food—that wishy-washy muck which the wife of the council-school's janitor cooks for them in the same cauldron she uses for the state convicts? Their palates—the tender and genial palates of fire-sprites—have need of the aromatic bouquet of colorful drinks. That is why, when we sit tonight among the bright lights and festive tables of the town hall, every man of us will dip his bun into a tumbler of raspberry juice and will sip that dark, noble liquor with a piety and relish which is peculiar to the race of fire-eaters. How else could the innards of firemen be able to belch forth like fireworks? My soul is filled with compassion at the sight of their misery and degradation. If I accepted the sword of captaincy, then I did so only in the hope that I would be able to save this race from its downfall, to lead it out of its plight and to unfurl the banner of a new ideology over its head."

"How much you have changed, Jacob," exclaimed my mother. "You really are magnificent! But all the same, you won't leave this house tonight. Don't forget that we haven't been able to have a chat together ever since I returned. And as for the firemen. . . ." At this point she turned to Adela. ". . . as for the firemen, I honestly do

think that you are being influenced by some sort of prejudice. For my part I must say that I always find pleasure
in looking at those slim young men in their handsome uni-
forms—a little too tight in the waist though they are—and
I really like the elegant and eager way in which they are
always ready to oblige a lady. If ever I drop my umbrella
in the street, or if my shoelace comes undone, there is always at least one of them who will come rushing along
to my assistance. I never have the heart to disappoint
them. If I were you, Adela, I would also gladly take ad-
vantage of their gallantry."

Theodore, the senior shop-assistant, said: "I regard
them all as parasites, particularly since we don't even allow them to try and put out fires because of their childish
irresponsibility. It's enough to see the way in which they'll
always join in a children's game of marbles to appreciate
the quality of their mentality. Whenever there's a commotion in the street you can bet your bottom dollar that
right in the middle of the crowd you'll see several of those
lanky creatures looking absolutely beside themselves with
excitement. At the very sight of a fire they go off their
heads with delight, dancing around like savages and clap-
ping their hands. And yet, when it comes to putting the
fire out, one simply can't trust them. Oh no, we have to use
chimney-sweeps and militiamen instead. The only time
when they're of any use is during carnivals and proces-
sions. What's more, towards the end of the autumn they
become idle and sluggish. They fall asleep on their feet,
and once the first snow has fallen they are nowhere to be
seen. I was once told by an old potter friend of mine that
they are to be found whenever chimneys are being repaired—curled up like chrysalids, with their scarlet uni-

forms and shining helmets—in every nook and cranny of the vent-holes. One has to pull them out by the ears and cart them off along the streets to their barracks. They amble along, their insides filled with the warm, sweet glue of raspberry juice, as if they were completely drunk; and they smile rather guiltily when people at the roadside pelt them with stones. . . ."

"Anyhow," said Adela with finality, "I won't let them have the juice. I won't go and ruin my complexion by cooking it on the kitchen stove just so that those good-for-nothing creatures can go and drink it all."

Instead of answering, my father raised a whistle to his lips and blew it shrilly. So quickly that it seemed they must have been listening at the keyhole, four slim young men rushed into the room and ranged themselves along the wall. They stood at attention in a military manner, looking dark and sunburned beneath their glittering helmets. At a signal from my father, two of them stepped briskly forward and grabbed the wicker handles of a large demijohn of raspberry juice, and before Adela was able to do anything to stop them they had made a hasty escape with their precious booty down the stairway. The two who remained gave a smart military salute and followed in the steps of their companions.

Adela's lovely eyes were suddenly filled with such a fire of fury that for a moment she seemed about to fly into an irresponsible rage. But my father did not wait for her outburst. With a single leap he jumped on to the window-sill and stood there with his arms outstretched. We all rushed after him. In the brightly illuminated square below us we could see a milling crowd of people; immediately beneath our window a group of eight firemen was stretching out an enormous sheet of canvas. Father turned around, sparkling in the glory of his apparel, and saluted us. Then, with his arms outflung, he leaped out into the glittering night like a blazing meteor. It was such a wonderful sight that we all clapped our hands in rapture, and even Adela forgot her temper enough to join us in our enthusiastic approval of such an elegant feat.

In the meantime my father had rebounded from the sheet like an India-rubber ball and, with a rattle of his crustacean brass, had placed himself at the head of a detachment of firemen, whose helmets sparkled as they marched in file through the ranks of applauding onlookers.

PIOTR CHOYNOWSKI (1885–1935) published a number of collections of short stories and also wrote a play *Ruchome piaski* (*Moving Sands*), 1913, and a novel *Kuźnia* (*The Forge*), 1919, which deals with the period 1861–63, the time of the insurrection against Russia. His forte was the short story in which he perfected a number of techniques.

HELEN JANKOWSKA, the translator, is secretary to the Department of History at Wayne State University and a major in Polish language and literature.

Boarding House

PIOTR CHOYNOWSKI

$\mathcal{T}$he silence typical of a Saturday afternoon reigns to-day in the professor's boarding house in Kielce. All the "gentlemen" of the upper classes have either gone home or gone into town. Only three boys remain in the big "studyroom": Wroblewski of the third class, Turowicz of the second, and little Chet of the first.

Turowicz and Chet are sitting at the ink-stained table and doing their homework for Monday. Turowicz, a book in his hand, is rocking back and forth on his chair and muttering something under his breath; at the same time he is chewing on large pieces of bread which he keeps pulling out of a tattered pocket. He's always eating; it's his nature; that's the way he is.

Chet, small and chubby, is copying Latin words into a small notebook, but this is going slowly for him. Even the assistance of a protruding tongue, which he knows is disgraceful, doesn't help his concentration. With every word he writes, he pauses and stares at the spattered table, like a cow at a fence. Tomorrow, he thinks, is Sunday, and he wonders whether mama will come from

Ojcow or not. From time to time, he glances furtively at *Mister* Wroblewski.

Mister Wroblewski—who has so instructed Chet respectfully to address him inasmuch as he is fourteen years old and this is his second year in the third class—isn't doing his homework. He has no time. He is preparing to shave. He has already brought the soap and shaving-brush from the room of Mr. Zdanowicz, who is in the eighth class, and is now sharpening his father's old razor. Katie, the maid, has refused to give him any hot water so *Mister* Wroblewski now proposes to shave with cold water. Shave he must, because tomorrow afternoon he is going to the movies to a showing especially for the youth.

Chet observes these preparations with an ironic eye. He doesn't say anything since *Mister* Wroblewski is a sturdy fellow and quite competent with his fists, but he knows very well that there is no reason to shave. Two blond hairs growing from a wart on the upper lip don't make a mustache. They could be cut with a scissors. But *Mister* Wroblewski claims they actually are a mustache and is raking his smooth cheeks with a blunt razor until it's uncomfortable to watch.

At this moment, Turowicz reaches into his torn pocket, finds nothing, and stops muttering. Rocking one more time, he inclines toward Chet the dark and terribly freckled face which has earned him the nicknames "Egg Yolk" and "Turkey Egg."

"Hey, Mama's boy! Got an apple?"

Chet practically explodes at this gluttony. The pig has eaten everything which mama brought the last time, and now he doesn't even remember. He mutters sullenly:

"No, I haven't."

Turowicz sighs.

"You never have anything. . . . Say, what's up today? When's supper?"

At this, he pridefully pulls out a real watch which has numbers that actually glow in the dark. He blows on it, wipes his sleeve over the glass, and finally announces solemnly:

"It's 7:30."

Chet didn't answer even with a word. He had become very thoughtful. He mused sadly that though he had been here a month and a half, he still hadn't got used to it. Actually, the professor's wife is very good to him, always giving him two portions of dessert, but what difference does this make? It's a thousand times better back home in Ojcow with mama. Furthermore, Chet can't stand it when they call him "Mama's boy."

It started like this. Chet arrived at the boarding house dressed in his Sunday best and wearing a blue, polka dot necktie. No sooner had *Mister* Wroblewski spotted him than he yanked at the end of the tie and said:

"You—who ties your necktie for you, baby?"

"Mommie."

"Well, get that! 'Mommie!' Turowicz, did you hear that? 'Mommie!' Mama's boy! Dope!"

And "Mama's boy" he remained. They even call him that in school. Chet is exasperated, for obviously everybody's mama ties his necktie for him! If Chet had a father, he would ask him how to deal with this "Mama's boy" question. But his father, a doctor, had died of typhoid during the war when Chet was still in diapers. And Mama probably would not understand. Besides, she has enough problems with the boarding house in Ojcow.

Suddenly, Chet is struck with a brilliant idea—he knows now what to do. He'll join the boy scouts! He'll ask mama for the green uniform, and he'll walk around in it, and if anyone sneers at him, he'll let him have one over the head; because scouts are brave so he, too, will be brave. Yes, he'll join the boy scouts. At the thought, Chet actually feels gay.

In the meantime, *Mister* Wroblewski had "shaved" one side of his face, and he calls on Chet to verify the fact:

"Hey, Mama's boy—com'ere. See, smooth, isn't it?"

Chet brushes his hand skeptically across *Mister* Wroblewski's face:

"It was smooth and is smooth."

Mister Wroblewski becomes very angry at this:

"Whad'ja mean—'it was smooth.' What are you talking about, dope? Mama's boy! Here's something to remember!"

And he rakes his fingernail across Chet's scalp from the forehead to the top of the head. Chet actually gasps from the pain.

"Don't start a fight now, because. . . ."

"Because what?"

"Nothing."

Chet would cheerfully have kicked his tormentor, but justice was done without any effort on his part and before *Mister* Wroblewski could even suspect. In the heat and anger of the moment, he begins to shave so quickly that the razor almost cuts off half his ear before he is aware of what has happened. He has cut himself thoroughly. The blood gushes. *Mister* Wroblewski becomes as white as a sheet and leaps to the basin, screaming at Chet in a loud voice:

"Mama's boy! The alum! Get the alum! Get going or I'll bleed to death! Oh, how it hurts!"

Chet, equally unnerved by the accident, asks curtly:

"Where is the alum?"

"On Mr. Staszewski's window-sill! I saw it. Run, for the love of God!"

Ha—it was easily said—"on Mr. Staszewski's window-sill!" But the whole boarding house is afraid to go into this room. Everyone knows from Katie that the professor's father had died there during the summer. And now, in addition, no one is home and it's dark. Chet quickly makes up his mind:

"I won't go. There are ghosts there."

"What ghosts! Go this minute!"

"I won't go. Go yourself."

Mister Wroblewski becomes angry again.

"How can I go with this towel over my ear? But perhaps, if two of you went. . . . Turowicz, will you go?"

Turowicz keeps rocking indifferently on his chair.

"Not a chance."

Mister Wroblewski becomes even angrier.

"Coward, Egg Yolk, Turkey Egg! I'll bleed to death! This is the kind of friendship we have! Mama's boy! Coward!"

The "Turkey Egg" doesn't bat an eyelash at this outburst. But the charge of cowardice strikes Chet to the heart. What kind of a scout will he be if he's afraid of a dark room? Either . . . or. He has to go—there's no way out. He has to go.

"All right. Just so you'll know, I'll go."

And he immediately goes down the corridor at a trot so it will be over with all the faster. Opening the door to the dark room, he screws up his eyes and peers through tiny slits so as to see as little as possible. His heart pounds like a hammer. A hazy streak of light from some lamp falls on the wall; it looks as if someone tall and transparent is standing there. Chet actually shudders. With shaking fingers, he feels along the window-sill—a glass, a toothbrush, a small box, something smooth and cold . . . alum? He licks it to be sure. Yes, it's the alum. Thank God. And suddenly, he is very calm. He now unhurriedly returns down the corridor, pleased and proud. He has been afraid, yet he has done what had to be done. Just like a scout, a real scout. Now he's on equal terms with *Mister* Wroblewski.

The blood from *Mister* Wroblewski's ear begins to congeal now. And he is his old self again.

"Oh, here is Mama's boy with the alum! Just in time! You should be sent out only to summon death! Give it to me!"

Chet relinquishes the alum, backs up to the table and remarks to *Mister* Wroblewski:

"You sure are a big coward. And I'm not going to call you *Mister* anymore. You're as much of a *Mister* as I am. Just an ordinary coward. I'm going to call you 'Sparrow' just like everybody else. Yes, Sparrow!"

Turowicz actually stops rocking in his astonishment. *Mister* Wroblewski at the wash basin is equally dumbfounded. And Chet continues:

"And if you start a fight, Sparrow, I'll throw this lamp at you and make a racket that'll be heard throughout the house. Now, you know!"

Mister Wroblewski hurls himself at Chet with a shout: "You think so?"

"I know so!"

Chet leaps to the other side of the table and actually seizes the oil lamp. This convinces *Mister* Wroblewski. He pants a while, angrily mutters something under his breath, and finally shrugs his shoulders:

"Dope, doesn't even know when I'm joking."

From that time on, Chet had no trouble with Mister Wroblewski. And he did join the boy scouts.

MARIA KUNCEWICZOWA (1897–   ) is well known to American and English readers as a novelist. Among her novels, *Cudzoziemka* (*The Stranger*), *Klucze* (*The Keys*), *Zmowa nieobecnych* (*The Conspiracy of the Absent*) and *Leśnik* (*The Forester*) have been translated into English. She is also a musician and makes notable use of musical, as well as color, elements in her writing. The short story collection *Dwa księżyce* (*Two Moons*), from which the following selection was taken, remains popular with Polish readers. Mrs. Kuncewiczowa now resides in this country.

GEORGE J. MACIUSZKO, the translator, a native Pole, is now assistant head of the Foreign Literature Department, Cleveland Public Library. He has contributed to Polish émigré periodicals in London and to professional journals in this country. In 1943, while a prisoner of war in German hands, he was awarded a prize by the International YMCA in Geneva for his short story "Koncert f-moll" ("Concerto in F Minor").

A Turban

MARIA KUNCEWICZOWA

$\mathcal{T}$he rain kept drizzling. A raw wind kept blowing from the river into the town, sniping at people. It was one of those annoying three-day summer rains with grayness so complete and the cold so ruthless and penetrating that it was difficult to recall the good weather breathing brightness and warmth some tens of hours earlier. Now it seemed like a dim vision in a narcotic dream.

Simon put on his windproof jacket and meandered out. When he arrived at the market place he found it quite deserted: only two porters were getting themselves officially wet while waiting for the bus near the well. The wife of the pharmacist, pulling at the sleeves of her sweater to cover the palms of her hands and peering out through the glass door of her store, watched a lonely hen strolling heroically on the slippery pavement. In contrast, homeless or idle townsfolk loitered or shifted from foot to foot in recesses, doorways, and under eaves. The rain was—for them—calamity or entertainment. It stripped the last bit of comfort from some. It sweetened extreme boredom for others. The homeless crouched and suffered, while the idle watched the eddying pools of water with the same dull interest with which they had watched spots of sunshine two days before.

Simon in his waterproof outfit waded aimlessly forward. Passing by the porters he looked around when he heard someone greeting him.

"How d'you do, sir. You seem to be headed for the telegraph office, sir. Is something wrong, God forbid?"

Moshek Ruchlingier shifted from foot to foot. His turned-up collar interfered with his beard, his hands were stuck in his pockets. He kept talking, his small bead-like eyes gleaming with anxiety. Behind the patience in his eyes lay suffering. It was obvious that at the moment he was cold and felt a stranger on this market place beside the Vistula.

Simon looked in turn at the other porter, Cackowski. This tall, slim man was leaning back against the railing of the well; his head, firmly placed on his stiff neck, was directed carelessly toward the clouds while drops of water fell down his cheeks and his chest from the visor of his porter's cap. Cackowski, however, was not showing any signs of discomfort and he was not trembling. Solidly poised in the mud, he gave the impression of a tree joyfully spreading out and up to receive friendly elements.

Simon shuddered. Suddenly he became keenly aware of how close his lot was to Moshek's: this shifting from foot to foot beside the unconquerable, strange trees. Despite his windproof jacket he was cold and felt a tremor of horror go through him. Through this climate he saw the world. The ties binding his family to Jerusalem were nothing more than a Biblical tradition. Who could tell if in Simon's system there was even one atom of Palestinian sunshine? But still these rainy August days were driving him on to the precipice of homelessness. And—oh shame! He felt no longing after the Orient. He longed to have the wet winds comb out his wooly curls and make them as straight as hemp, to have the cold chill and narrow his eyes. He longed after a more natural place for himself somewhere in a corner of the spacious Slavic fields.

He muttered something in reply to Moshek and then moved on. The absurdity of his own desires made every one of his thoughts disgusting. He recalled reluctantly his last telegram to his mother:

> 15 Zamenhof Street, Warsaw. Mrs. Chaja Gold-
> man. First Prize in landscape competition.
> > Much love, Simon.

Now his prize-winning painting appeared to him a horrible forgery. Those birch trees, marsh marigolds, and the shepherd! The creative work of Chaja Goldman's son, of 15 Zamenhof Street! Just at that moment there emerged from behind the corner of the tannery the head and then the trunk of the body of a brindled cow. The herd was returning from pasture. Simon turned his back. He could not stand looking at the boy who bore indifferently his shepherd's bliss over real meadows, a bliss denied to Jewish shepherds.

He turned into a side street. As he did so he had to force his way against the wind. He trudged along with difficulty, whistling, and deriding himself because of the clash between his body and his environment. His face was that of an Afro-Asian hybrid, wide-nosed, thick-lipped with a smile which seemed cut out with the blade of a sharp knife; his hands were swarthy, his figure heavy set—all these features seemed to anger Boreas himself. The young man blinked his stiff eyelashes and decided to return, especially since Jeremy had promised to come this noon for a friendly discussion on art.

Near the store a door suddenly squeaked, opening over the sidewalk. A girl came down the steps of the shop and ran down the street. Her arm brushed Simon's side as she trudged across the muddy pavement. It was Madzia, the actress. He could see her profile and observe how carefully she skipped the mud by jumping on slim legs from one stone to another. He did not know her personally though he had often seen her about town. Heretofore he had not noticed any of the young girl's characteristics except that when she happened to be near him his heart would stop beating for a fraction of a second, and then it would thump. Still later, at night, he would dream heavy, enchanting, intoxicating dreams. Now at long last, despite the usual reaction in his chest, he could take a thorough look at her. Over her forehead the wind played with a streak of extremely fine and fair hair, while her eyes, pale as smoke, appeared to be without iris or frame. They were simply a gaze which expressed an aimless and a boundless sorrow. Her figure, or rather, her lines could not be easily distinguished, as they were all one with her fluid movements. But Madzia's nose was clearly bluish and her cheeks blue from the cold. Rather than walk she seemed to soar on the damp air, held in suspension by the secret of this rainy day whose essence was so completely entrusted to her.

Simon hurried home as quickly as he could. Jeremy was already there waiting for him. It goes without saying that there was no discussion on art. In his desire to know more about Madzia, Simon began a philosophical discussion in order to be able to talk about women with his older, usually reserved, colleague. Somehow Jeremy became interested in the discussion which, in turn, was followed by light anecdotes, and before long Simon got out of him some stories about Madzia. They were all to her credit. She was an independent person. Her talents made up for a lack of natural beauty, and her love affairs were all well chosen and discreet. She had, however, one queer trait. Whenever she played the part of somebody's mistress at the playhouse she would spread dark makeup all over herself.

Simon began to dream about conquering Madzia. He had no idea, though, how to go about it. Above all he did not know how to cover up nor how to adorn his all too-evident Jewishness.

The rainy weather was soon over and the visitors again returned to the beach. Since Simon had become aware of his love for the pale actress he was afraid to go there. He was tortured by the thought that even at this very moment Paul was sprawling on the sand beside Madzia, his heavy, white body close to her misty, snow-white flesh. He could see them rubbing cream on their arms and thighs, and then shading their eyes to estimate the strength of the sun, as though it were a healing lamp. Those children of the August rain and of the April snow! Now they are probably swimming, while lapwings cry something to them which only they understand. The splashing water murmurs some confidential secrets to them; then they dash back to the shore and wring out the water from their soft, fair hair. A couple of cold-blooded blonds! A couple in their native habitat. A couple not driven out of Paradise.

Simon walked about his rented room, flashing his nakedness in mirrors and laughing. What else but a laughing stock was this Jewish sample of a man on this flaxen river?

One morning Simon was looking through his suitcases in search of a blue tie. (Blue had a softening effect upon his features.) He could not find the tie but came across a richly embroidered silk scarf. It had come as a sample of still-life with a case of grapefruit sent him by a friend from Tel Aviv. Simon passionately wrapped himself a turban over his curls. Now there at last was something for him, an attire of attires! He reached for the mirror. The bright head of a native of Yemen looked back at him. Angrily he bared his teeth—the head laughed a monstrous, ghostly laugh. Simon pushed the mirror away and, trembling with inspiration, jumped to the wardrobe, grabbed his linen working pants and put them on as fast as he could. With undiminished speed he put on a dirty, colored shirt. He rolled up the sleeves, pushed his turban acock and stuck a pipe between his teeth. He now for all the world looked exactly like an Arabian porter. Once again he showed his teeth in a grin and with this Mohammedan smile he ran to the landing.

Old Shulim, the boatman, was instantly taken aback by the metamorphosis. Bashfully he turned his eyes away. Several girls who were already seated in the old skiff when Simon jumped in looked at each other in amazement and got out.

Around the island as usual, there was much splashing of water and hustle and bustle permeated with the odor

of osier and the beauty parlor. Flora, dressed in a huge
sun hat, walked along the edge of the beach. Mena, holding arrows in the air (the bow lay not far from her),
called Barbara's greyhound so that, beside the huge animal, she would look more like Diana. Sylvia and Jeremy
were paddling a canoe and singing, "Rrrum-bus the glo-
rious dance of great Colum-bus. . . ." On the syllable
"bus" their paddles struck the water simultaneously. Paul
and Gigi were waving their feet in the air. Madzia stood
beside them and struck their calves with a rod whenever
they bent their knees. The summer residents flocked in
the water and crowded the beach. They peeped at the
artists and gossiped about them. They made fools of themselves attempting to dazzle them.

Simon had made an impression. His friends surrounded
him.

"Hello," they cried. "Simeon! We like you in this little
costume! How did you manage to get yourself up as such
a Mohammedan apparition? It's true, 'a grandma is no
longer a grandmother and a Jew is no longer Jewish!' "

Singing this song they led the Arab to the ladies.

A few days later Simon, his bliss almost making him ill,
made a date with Madzia. He was to come to her. Alone.
There were to be just the two of them. He . . . and the
Slavic nebula.

And the afternoon had come. Simon, filled with de-
lirious feelings, began to dress. He ran around the room.
He kept muttering. He delighted in the few words which
Madzia pronounced as though she were speaking Russian.
She did not even say "Wyspianski" but "Wishpianski."
From her narrow, childish lips these words flowed so
gracefully. . . . Simon was dying of the wish that today

she would wear no lipstick. Let her lips be pale. Let them yield, their strength gone, in a kiss. Let them tremble with pain. Let her fair eyelids flutter on her white cheeks.

The feeling of sweetness overwhelmed the painter. After three mornings on the beach he had learned by heart even the smallest veins on Madzia's hips and all the intonations of her voice. Now he was to drink the very essence of her femininity.

He put on his saffron shirt, crumpled it and opened it deep on his chest, and at last, flashing a smile, he walked out abruptly, like a storm.

Madzia lived in a hut in a large plum orchard owned by some fishermen. It was there that Goldman had seen her the first time. She stood then with Paul among the plum trees. Down below shone the river. On the sides, nets were perched on poles to dry. They looked so harmonious, so simple, so happy, like two healthy stems of the same plant. It was then that Simon had begun to hate Paul—and himself.

But now everything was different. The turban had changed the ugly strangeness into a miracle. Now the man of Yemen was able to reach for what had been a vain dream not only of Chaja's son (15 Zamenhof Street) but also of the blue-eyed Paul of Kujawy.

Simon walked with large strides across the market place. Two boys ran behind him, shouting:

"You nigger! Tell us how far it is to hell? Look at him, a Turk! Give us some halvah, you disease!"

Then they fell to quarreling, trying to figure out who that fellow with a towel on his head could be.

Simon stopped at the gate. He sighed deeply. He was almost faint with tenderness. Now . . . in half a minute he would be grasping her pearly hand in his swarthy paw. In a half hour . . . perhaps . . . he would be pressing the breasts of this siren of the Vistula with his heavy, brown body. And then at last he would be able to throw away his hated Arab pretense. After having cheated away the antisemitic prejudice, he would be able to kiss this flaxen girl and weep with her in wonderful, all-human bliss.

He pushed the gate. Once again desire filled his veins. Simon ran through the orchard and reached the hut.

Near the steps to the porch he suddenly halted. . . . On the banister, perched like a bird on the branch of a tree, sat a wild woman. Feathers fluttered round her head; wild colors flared on her body. Abashed, he hurried to bypass the spectacle. Then, however, the woman jumped down from the banister and barred his way.

He looked . . . and was dumbfounded. It was Madzia —the actress. From under the black eyelids, thick with mascara, Simon felt her eyes rapaciously boring into him. The whites of her eyes and her teeth gleamed in the chestnut colored face, while her bare arms and legs tensed like straps of dark leather.

Simon groaned!

"What's this? What is this?"

Madzia replied, "It's me . . . my true self. I can't stand insipid beauty. Mine is purely exterior, accidental. Inside I feel I am a dark, wild woman."

Then she added passionately, "You are fond of me, aren't you? And you are also a fierce, splendid and exotic man. For you I want to be beautiful and my own true self!"

Simon was silent. He felt a painful emptiness replacing

143

his blissful passion. He broke into laughter. Then he shuffled his feet. At last, hardly able to speak, he said:

"A terrific, wild couple . . . indeed. Shouldn't we go to have a picture taken? It would be a fine vacation souvenir!"

WITOLD GOMBROWICZ (190?–   ) is one of the most controversial of modern Polish writers. The recent reprinting of his early novel *Ferdydurke* (an untranslatable title) in Poland caused no less a critical storm than when it first appeared. Gombrowicz now lives in Argentina. His writings appear frequently in the Paris *Kultura*. Among them have been a novel *Transatlantyk* (*Transatlantic*) whose technique recalls *Ferdydurke* and the continuing *Fragmenty z dziennika* (*Fragments from a Journal*). In the following short story, "Premeditated Crime," the reader will find the expression "examining magistrate." In Polish legal practice, specially chosen judges prepare unusually complicated or important cases. These "examining magistrates" perform some of the functions of a one-man grand jury, but they do not themselves judge the cases they have prepared.

OLGA SCHERER-VIRSKI, the translator, was born in Poland and is now on the faculty of Yale University. She is the author of *The Modern Polish Short Story* and has translated various Polish and French works into English. Mrs. Scherer-Virski, as the reader is already aware, has also written the Introduction to this volume.

Premeditated Crime

WITOLD GOMBROWICZ

*D*uring the winter of last year I had to visit the home of the country gentleman Mr. Ignace K. in order to help him settle some questions of property. Having obtained a few days' furlough, I entrusted my duties to my colleague, the assessor, and I wired: "Tuesday—6 p.m. please send horses." Yet when I arrived at the station there were no horses. I made inquiries; my telegram had been duly delivered. The addressee had called for it personally the day before. Willy-nilly I had to hire a primitive hack, load my suitcase and overnight bag on it—in the overnight bag I had a small bottle of cologne, a bottle of Vegetal, a cake of almond-scented toilet soap, a nail-file and scissors. I was knocked about in the hack for four hours, through the fields, at night, in silence and during a thaw. I shivered in my city overcoat, my teeth chattered. I watched the cabby's back and thought: "To risk one's back like this! Always to sit, frequently in a deserted region, with one's back turned and exposed to any whim on the part of those sitting behind."

At last we drove up in front of a wooden country house.

Darkness, except on the upper story where there was a lighted window. I knocked at the door; it was shut. I knocked harder—nothing but silence. The watchdogs attacked me, and I had to retreat. Now in turn my cabby tried to get in.

"Not very hospitable," I thought.

Finally the door opened, and a tall, slender man of about thirty, with a fair mustache and a lamp in his hand, appeared.

"What's that?" he asked, as though he had just awakened, lifting the lamp.

"Haven't you received my telegram? I am H."

"H.? What H.?" said he, staring at me. "May God be with you on your way," he suddenly said softly, as though he had just been struck by an omen; his eyes shot back and forth, while his hand pressed harder around the lamp. "Good-bye, good-bye, sir, God be with you!" and he hurriedly backed inside.

I said more sharply:

"Excuse me, sir. Yesterday I sent a telegram announcing my arrival. I am the examining magistrate, Judge H. I wish to see Mr. K., and if I couldn't come earlier, it's because no horses had been sent for me to the station."

He put the lamp away.

"Oh yes," he answered after a while, pondering. My tone had made no impression on him. "Yes, that's right; you did send a wire. Please come in."

What had happened? Just simply this, as the young man in the hall (who was the host's son) explained to me, they had simply . . . completely forgotten about both my arrival and the wire received the day before in the morning. Embarrassed, I politely apologized for my invasion, took off my coat and hung it on a hanger. He led me to a small sitting-room, where, upon seeing us, a young woman jumped from the sofa with a slight "Ah!". "My sister."—"Oh, delighted!" And delighted indeed, for femininity, even when no additional intentions are contemplated, femininity, I say, can never do any harm. But the hand she stretched out was perspiring—who ever heard of stretching a perspiring hand out to a man?—and, as for femininity itself, in spite of a charming face, it was kind of, shall I say, perspiring and indifferent, devoid of any reaction, untidy and uncombed.

We took our seats upon red, old-fashioned little pieces of furniture, and the introductory conversation began. But even the first, polite small talk met with undefinable resistance, and, instead of a desired fluency, everything broke and got stuck. I: "You must have been surprised to hear the knock on the door at this hour." They: "Knock? Oh yes, that's right. . . ." I, politely: "I am sorry to have disturbed you, but I would have had to ride in the fields all night, like Don Quixote, ha, ha!" They (still and quiet, not deeming it suitable to greet my little joke with as much as a conventional smile): "But, please, you are most welcome." What was it? It all looked really strange, as though they felt insulted, or as though they were afraid of me or sorry for me, or else as though they were ashamed for me. Squeezed into their chairs, they avoided my glance; they did not look at one another either and bore my company with the highest degree of reluctance. It seemed as though, preoccupied with no one but themselves, they kept trembling lest I should say something that might hurt them. This finally began to irritate me. What were they afraid of, what was so strange about me?

149

What kind of a reception was this: aristocratic, terrified and haughty? When I inquired about the object of my visit, namely Mr. K., the brother looked at his sister, the sister at her brother, as though they were giving each other priority. Finally the brother swallowed and said clearly, clearly and solemnly, as though this were God knows what: "Oh yes, he is at home."

It was just as if he were saying: "The King, my Father, is at home."

The dinner was also somewhat odd. It was served negligently, not without contempt for the food, as well as for me. The appetite with which, famished as I was, I swept up God's gifts, seemed shocking even to the majestic valet Szczepan, not to speak of the brother and sister, who silently listened to the noises I produced over my plate, and you know how hard it is to swallow when someone is listening; in spite of yourself every mouthful falls into your throat with a dreadful gurgle. The brother's Christian name was Anthony, his sister's—Cecilia.

Then all of a sudden, who came in? A deposed queen? No, it was the mother, Mrs. K. She moved slowly, stretched out a hand as cold as ice, glanced around her with a suggestion of dignified astonishment and sat down without a word. She was a plump person, short, even fat, belonging to the type of country matrons who are inexorable where principles are concerned, especially principles of social life; she looked at me with severity and boundless surprise, as though I had an indecent slogan written out on my forehead. Cecilia made a movement with her hand which attempted to explain or to justify, but the movement died out in midair, while the atmosphere became even heavier and more artificial.

"You are probably displeased about this unsuccessful trip," Mrs. K. suddenly said, but with what a tone! A wounded tone, the tone of a queen who failed to receive the third of a series of bows, and as though the eating of chops constituted a *crimen laesae maiestatis.*

"You have excellent pork chops here," I said with rancor, for in spite of myself, I felt vulgarity, stupidity, embarrassment rising in me gradually.

"The chops, the chops. . . ."

"Tony has not said anything yet, mother," was all that shot out of the mouth of the quiet, timid Cecilia.

"What's that? He hasn't? What do you mean, you haven't said anything? You *still* haven't said anything?"

"What for, mother?" Anthony whispered, turned pale and set his teeth as though he were settling down in a dentist's chair.

"Tony. . . ."

"Oh well . . . what for? It doesn't matter. . . . Never mind. . . . There'll always be time for that," he said and stopped.

"Tony, how can you, what do you mean, never mind? How can you talk like this, Tony?"

"It's nobody's. . . . It's all the same. . . ."

"You poor thing," the mother whispered, stroking his hair, but he rudely pushed her hand away. "My husband," she said dryly, addressing me, "died last night." What? He died? So that's why! I stopped eating. I put my knife and fork aside and quickly swallowed the mouthful I held in my mouth. How could that be? Only yesterday he had received my wire at the station! I looked at them. All three waited, modestly and gravely, but they waited with austere, closed, set mouths. They waited stiffly. What were they waiting for? Oh yes, of course, I should express my condolences.

This was so unexpected that in the first moment I completely lost my self-control. I rose from my chair confused and mumbled something indistinctly like this: "I am sorry . . . very . . . forgive me." I stopped, but they did not react; this was not enough for them. With their eyes cast down, their faces still, their clothes shabby, he—unshaven, they—ungroomed, with dirty fingernails, they stood saying nothing. I cleared my throat, desperately looking for a suitable opening, an appropriate phrase, but in my head, you know the feeling, there was a complete vacuum, a desert, while, plunged in suffering, they waited. They waited without looking up, Anthony lightly knocking his fingers on the table, Cecilia with embarrassment picking the hem of her dirty dress, and the mother, motionless, as though turned to stone, with that severe, unyielding matron's expression. I felt uncomfortable, although after all, as an examining magistrate, I have handled hundreds of cases of death. But it was just that . . . how shall I say it: an ugly murdered corpse, covered with a blanket, is one thing, and the respectable deceased who dies a natural death and is placed on a catafalque, quite another. A certain informality (which accompanies the former) is one thing, but honest death, death, as it were, in all its majesty, is quite another. Never, I repeat, never, would I have felt so embarrassed, had they told me everything right away. But they felt too uncomfortable. They were too afraid. I do not know whether it was simply because I was an intruder or else because, in these circumstances, they experienced embarrassment in the face of my official status, in face of a certain matter-of-fact attitude that my long practice must have developed in me; in any case, this shame of theirs made me feel terribly ashamed somehow; frankly speaking, it made me feel ashamed quite out of proportion.

I stammered something about the respect and affection I had always had for the dead man. Remembering that I had not met him since our school days, a fact which they might have known, I added: "in our school days." As they still did not answer, and as I had somehow to finish, to round out the edges, and not finding anything to add, I asked: "May I see the body?" and the word "body" made an unfortunate sound. My confusion obviously appeased the widow. She broke into tears painfully and gave me her hand which I humbly kissed.

"Today," she said half-consciously, "during the night. . . . in the morning I get up . . . I come in . . . I call: Ignace, Ignace—nothing; he just lies there. I fainted . . . I fainted. . . . And my hands have been trembling ever since. There, look at them!"

"Mother, why?"

"They keep trembling, trembling all the time." She flung her arms up.

"Mother," Anthony said again from the side in a soft voice.

"They tremble, tremble, tremble all on their own, like an aspen. . . ."

"It's nobody's . . . nobody . . . it's all the same. A disgrace!" He pushed the words out of himself brutally and turned around abruptly. He left. "Tony," the mother cried fearfully, "Cecilia, go after him." And there I stood, looking at the trembling hands and I had nothing at all to say and I felt that I was losing myself and getting more embarrassed by the minute.

Suddenly the widow quietly said: "You wished to. . . . Let us go . . . there . . . I shall lead you." Today, considering the whole affair coldly, I basically believe that at that moment I had a right to my own person and to my pork chops, that is, I could have, and even should have, answered: "At your service, Madam, but first I will finish my chops because I have not eaten anything since noon." Perhaps if I had answered thus, the course of several tragic events might have turned. But was it my fault that she succeeded in terrorizing me so that the chops, as well as my own person, appeared to me as petty and unworthy of thought? And I was suddenly so embarrassed that to this day I blush at the thought of that embarrassment.

On our way to the upper floor where the deceased was resting she whispered to herself:

"A terrible shock. . . . A blow, an awful blow. They didn't say anything. They are proud, difficult, inscrutable, they don't let anyone into their hearts, they prefer to be crushed all alone. They take after me. After me. . . . Oh, I hope Tony doesn't do himself any harm! He is hard and obstinate; he won't even let my hands tremble. He wouldn't have the body touched, and yet we should have decided to do something, made arrangements. He didn't cry, he didn't cry at all. Oh, how I wish he would weep but once!"

She opened a door. I had to kneel and bow my head with concentration on my face, while she stood at my side, solemn, motionless, as though she were revealing the most Holy Sacrament to me.

The dead man lay on the bed just as he had died; all

they had done was to place him on his back. His blue, swollen face indicated death by suffocation, as usual in heart attacks.

"Choked to death," I whispered, though I clearly saw that it had been a heart attack.

"It's the heart, the heart. . . . He died of the heart. . . ."

"Oh, sometimes the heart can choke you . . . it can," I said grimly. She continued to stand, waiting. So, crossing myself, I said a prayer and then (she was still standing) I softly said:

"Noble features!"

Her hands trembled so that I really should have kissed them again. She did not react with the slightest gesture, but continued to stand, like a cypress, staring painfully at the wall, and the longer she stood like this, the harder it was to avoid manifesting at least a little compassion. Simple decency demanded it, and one could not get out of it. I rose from my knees, unnecessarily brushed some lint from my suit and coughed quietly; she was still standing. She stood in silence and oblivion, her eyes staring vacantly, like Niobe, with her glance nailed to memories. She was disheveled and unkempt; a small drop appeared at the end of her nose and it dangled, dangled . . . like the sword of Damocles, while the candles smoked. A few minutes later I tried to break away quietly; she jumped up, as though she had been stung, made a few steps forward and stopped short again. I knelt down. What an unbearable situation! What a dilemma for a sensitive person like me. I do not accuse her of conscious malice. Nobody could convince me of that! It was not she, but her malice that insolently enjoyed my practices of humility before her and the corpse.

On my knees, two steps away from the corpse, the first corpse I was unable to touch, I stared fruitlessly at the blanket which covered him smoothly to the armpits, at the hands folded on top of the blanket; potted plants stood at the foot of the bed, and the face emerged pallidly from the hollow of the pillow. I looked at the flowers and then I looked again at the deceased man's face, but nothing came to my head except the one importunate, strangely obstinate thought that this was a kind of prearranged theatrical scene. Everything appeared stage-like: over there—a corpse, haughty, unapproachable, indifferently staring at the ceiling with his closed eyes; next to him—his suffering widow; and over here—myself, an examining magistrate, on his knees but with an utterly empty heart, furious as a dog which had been forced to wear a muzzle. "How about getting up, going closer, removing the blanket and taking a look, at least touching, touching with one finger?" This is what I was thinking, but the grave honesty of death nailed me down, and suffering and virtue kept me from profanation. Away! Forbidden! Don't you dare! On your knees! What was it? I gradually began to wonder who had staged it all like this. I was a simple, ordinary man and I did not fit into such performances. . . . I would not. . . . "To hell!" I suddenly thought: "What nonsense! How could this happen to me? Could it be that I am putting things on? Where do I get such artificiality, such affectation? After all, I am usually quite different. Perhaps I have caught the bug from them? What is this? Ever since my arrival everything I do comes out artificial, pretentious, like the performance of a mediocre actor. I have completely lost my personality in this house, I am putting on airs."

"Hm," I whispered again, not without a certain theatrical pose (as though I were already pulled into the game and unable to regain hold of my normal self). "I wouldn't advise anyone . . . I wouldn't advise anyone to make a demon out of me, for I would be capable of accepting the challenge." In the meantime the widow wiped her nose and started towards the door, talking to herself, clearing her throat and waving her arms.

When I finally found myself in my room, I took off my collar, but, instead of putting it on the table, I threw it on the floor and then even crushed it with my foot. My face twisted and reddened with blood, and my fingers stiffened tensely in a way which was entirely unexpected. I must have been furious. "They ridiculed me," I whispered, "what a vicious woman! How cleverly they arranged everything! They want homage . . . their hands kissed! They demand my feelings! Feelings! They want to be fussed about! And let us suppose that I cannot stand feeling. Let us suppose that I hate to be forced to kiss hands just because they tremble or to mumble prayers, to kneel down, to produce false sounds, horribly sentimental sounds, and above all I hate tears and drops which dangle at the tips of noses; on the other hand, I do like cleanliness and order."

"Hm," I cleared my throat deliberately, using a different tone of voice, carefully, as though I were just trying, "they want to have their hands kissed? I should perhaps kiss their feet, for after all, who am I before the majesty of death and this familial suffering? A vulgar, insensitive cop, nothing more. My nature showed itself. But . . . ha . . . I don't know . . . wasn't it a little too hasty? In their position I, personally, would have been somewhat

more . . . careful, just a trifle more . . . modest. Because they should have taken into account this miserable
character of mine, and if not my . . . private character,
then . . . then . . . at least my official character. This,
they have forgotten. After all, I am an examining magistrate, and there is a corpse here, and the concept of corpse
somehow seems to rhyme, not altogether innocently, with
the concept of examining magistrate. And if we were to
consider the course of events from that point of view . . .
hm . . . the point of view of an examining magistrate,"
I slowly kept formulating, "what would the outcome be?"

Look at it this way: a guest arrives, who, quite by accident, is an examining magistrate. They do not send any
horses, they do not open the door. In other words, he is
being made to feel uncomfortable; hence, it is in someone's interest not to let this man into the house. Then he
is received reluctantly, with poorly concealed anger, with
fear, and who would be afraid, who would be angry at
the sight of an examining magistrate? Something was
being kept from him, concealed. A man who died as the
result of choking in a room upstairs. Not nice! As soon as
the corpse came to light they used every means to force
you to kneel, to kiss hands under the pretext that the
deceased had died a natural death.

Anyone who would call this reasoning absurd or even
ridiculous (for, after all, frankly speaking, how far can
you go in fooling people?), let him not forget that only
a moment earlier I had crushed my collar on the floor. My
accountability was decreased, my consciousness dimmed
as a result of the insult; it is clear that I could not be fully
responsible for my whims.

Looking straight ahead, I said in all seriousness: "Something is not in order."

And with all my sharpness I began to piece together the chain of facts, to build syllogisms, to draw threads and to look for evidence. Yes, yes, the majesty of death is by all means worthy of respect, and no one will say that I did not render it the honors it deserved, but not every kind of death is equally majestic.

"And before this circumstance has been cleared up, I would not, in their position, be so sure of myself, especially since the case is obscure, complex and doubtful, hm . . . hm . . . as all evidence seems to indicate."

The next morning, drinking coffee in bed, I noticed that the servant-boy, who was making a fire in the stove, a squat, sleepy youth, glanced at me from time to time with a weak glimmer of curiosity. He probably knew who I was, and so I spoke to him:

"So your master is dead?"

"Quite so."

"How large is the staff here?"

"There is Szczepan and the chef, Your Honor. Excluding me. Including me, there are three of us."

"The master died in the room upstairs?"

"Upstairs, of course," he replied indifferently, blowing at the fire and puffing up his fleshy cheeks.

"And where do you sleep?"

He stopped blowing and glanced at me, but his glance was sharper this time.

"Szczepan sleeps with the chef in a room by the kitchen, and I sleep alone in the pantry."

"That means that from the place where Szczepan and

the chef sleep there is no way of going to the rooms except through the pantry?" I kept inquiring, as though unintentionally.

"None," he replied and looked at me quite sharply now.

"And where does your mistress sleep?"

"Until recently with the master, and now in a room next to his."

"Since his death?"

"Oh no, she moved out earlier than that, a week ago maybe."

"And do you happen to know why your mistress moved out of her husband's room?"

"Don't know. . . ."

I asked one more question: "And where does the young master sleep?"

"On the ground floor, next to the dining room."

I got up and dressed carefully. "Hm . . . hm. . . . Well, if I am not mistaken, I have found another significant item of evidence, an interesting detail. After all, it is astonishing why one week before her husband's death the lady should leave their bedroom. Was she afraid of catching a heart disease? This would have been a superfluous fear, to say the least. Let us not come to any premature conclusions, however, nor make any hasty moves!" And I went down to the dining room. The widow stood by the window; with her hands laced together, she stared at a coffee cup and whispered something monotonously, zealously shaking her head, a dirty, wet handkerchief in her hands. When I came up closer she suddenly began to walk around the table in the opposite direction, continuing to whisper, waving an arm, as though she had lost her senses, but I had already regained the poise I had lost the day before and, stepping aside, I patiently waited until she finally took notice of me.

"Ah, good-bye, good-bye, sir," she said vacuously, seeing my repeated bows. "I was delighted. . . ."

"Sorry," I whispered, "I . . . I . . . am not yet leaving. I should like to stay a little longer. . . ."

"Oh, it's you," she said. She mumbled something about the removal of the body and even honored me by asking faintly whether I would stay to attend the funeral.

"That is a great honor," I said reverently. "Who could refuse this last service? Will I be allowed to visit the dear body once more?" Without a reply and without looking around to see whether I was following, she stepped on the creaking stairs.

After a brief prayer, I rose to my feet and, as though pondering on the riddle of life and death, I looked around me. "It's strange," I said to myself, "interesting." Judging by the evidence, this man certainly died a natural death. Although his face was swollen and livid, like that of a person strangled, there were absolutely no traces of violence anywhere, neither on the body, nor in the room. It really seemed that he might have died quietly of a heart attack. Yet I came closer to the bed and touched his neck with my finger.

This trifling movement acted on the widow like lightning. She jumped.

"What's this?" she cried. "What's this? What's this?"

"Please do not get upset, my dear madam," I replied and, without any further fuss, I examined the corpse's neck, as well as the whole room, in detail. Making a fuss is fine for a time. But we would not get very far if scruples prevented us from carrying through a detailed inspection when the need arises. Alas! Still literally no traces of any kind. None on the body, none on the dresser, behind the wardrobe or on the rug by the bed. The only object worthy of attention was an immense dead cockroach. However, a certain trace appeared on the widow's face; she stood still, observing my activities with an expression of hazy terror.

I therefore asked her as cautiously as I could: "Why did you move to your daughter's room a week ago?"

"I? Why? I? Why did I move? How dare. . . . My son talked me into it . . . for more air. My husband had been choking at night. But how can. . . . After all, what business? . . . what do you . . . ?"

"Please forgive me. I am sorry, but. . . ." A significant silence supplied the rest of the sentence.

She manifested some understanding, as though she had suddenly realized the official status of the person she was addressing.

"But, after all . . . how can it be? But you, but you certainly . . . didn't notice anything?"

The sound of undisguised fear rang in her question. I only cleared my throat in reply. "Whatever the case," I said dryly, "may I ask you . . . you said something about removing the body. . . . Well, I must ask you to leave the body here until tomorrow morning."

"Ignace!" she exclaimed.

"That's just it," I replied.

"Ignace! How can that be? Incredible, impossible," she said with a dull glance at the body. "My little Ignace!"

And, interestingly, she stopped short in the middle of a word, stiffened and crushed me with her glance, after which, deeply insulted, she left the room. I ask you, what is there to feel insulted about? Does a man's unnatural death constitute an insult to his wife, if she did not have a share in it? What is insulting about unnatural death? Granted, it may be insulting to the murderer, but certainly never to the corpse or his relatives? But for the time being I had something more urgent to do than to formulate rhetorical questions. Left alone with the corpse, I again began my detailed examination, but the longer I conducted it, the greater was my astonishment. "Nothing, nothing at all," I whispered, "nothing besides the cockroach behind the dresser. One might indeed suppose that there was no basis for any further action."

Well, that was the trouble! The corpse himself, who loudly and distinctly proved to the expert's eye that he had died normally in a heart attack. All the appearances—the horses, the reluctance, the fear and concealment—argued for something unclear, but the corpse, staring at the ceiling, announced: "I died of a heart attack!" It was a physical and medical certainty, it was a fact; he had not been murdered by anyone for the simple and conclusive reason that he was not murdered at all. I had to admit that the majority of my colleagues in the profession would have suspended the inquest right there and then. Not I! I felt too ridiculous, too vindictive and I had already pushed ahead too far. I raised a finger and wrinkled my brow. Murder does not come by itself, gentlemen, murder has to be worked out intellectually, it has to be thought over, thought out. Roast pigeons don't fly through the air.

"When appearances testify against the murder," I said wisely, "we must be cunning, we must not be caught by the appearances. If, on the other hand, logic, common sense and evidence finally become the criminal's advocate, and appearances speak against him, let us not trust logic or evidence. All right . . . but with all the appearances, how can we—as Dostoevskij says—prepare a roast of hare without having the hare?" I looked at the corpse, and the corpse looked at the ceiling, his neck proclaiming immaculate innocence. Therein lay the difficulty! Therein lay the obstacle! But what cannot be removed must be jumped over: *hic Rhodus, hic salta.* Was it possible for this frozen face to put up any resistance against my quick, changing physiognomy, which was capable of finding a suitable expression for any situation? And while the corpse's face remained the same—calm, though somewhat swollen—my face expressed solemn cunning, a stupid conceit and assurance of self, just as if I were saying: "I am too old a bird to be caught with chaff."

"Yes," I said gravely, "an obvious fact: the man was choked to death."

The caviling of the legal profession would perhaps try to claim that he was choked to death by the heart. Hm . . . hm . . . I couldn't be fooled by the defense. The heart is a very broad concept, we might even say, a symbolic concept. Who, after rising with fury at the news of a crime, will be satisfied to hear the appeasing reply that it was nothing, that the heart had done the choking? Excuse me, what heart? We know how confused, how complex a heart can be. A heart is a sack which can hold a lot of things: the cold heart of a murderer, the libertine's heart reduced to ashes, the faithful heart of a woman in love, an ardent heart, an ungrateful heart, a jealous heart, a vengeful heart, etc.

The crushed cockroach did not appear to remain in

direct connection with the crime. So far one thing had been settled: the deceased was choked to death and the choking was of a cardiac nature. Considering the lack of any external injuries, one could also state that the choking had a typically internal character. Yes, that was all . . . nothing further; an internal, cardiac character. "Let us be wary of premature conclusions, and now it would be good to take a little walk around the house."

I returned downstairs. Upon entering the dining room, I heard the sound of light, quickly fleeing footsteps, probably Cecilia's. "Oh, it's not good to run away, little girl; truth always pursues." Passing by the dining room, whence, setting the table for dinner, the servants watched me stealthily, I slowly ventured into more distant rooms, when somewhere in the doorway I caught a glimpse of Anthony's fleeing back. Speaking of an internally caused death, of a cardiac type, I pondered, one must admit that no house lent itself to it better than did this old dwelling. Strictly speaking, there was perhaps nothing distinctly incriminating, and yet—I sniffed—and yet there was panic, and a certain specific odor in the air, an odor of the kind you can stand when it is your own, such as the odor of perspiration, an odor which I would designate as the odor of family affections. Still sniffing around, I noted certain little details, which, though slight, did not seem to me without significance. Thus, the faded, yellowed curtains, the hand-embroidered cushions, the abundance of photographs and portraits, the backs of chairs caved in by the backs of many generations, and, besides these, an interrupted letter on white lined paper, a piece of butter on a knife in one of the sitting-room windows, a glass with medicine on a dresser, a blue ribbon behind a stove, a cobweb, many wardrobes, old smells—all these constituted an atmosphere of particular solicitude, of great cordiality. At every step the heart encountered food for itself; yes, the heart could go to town on old butter, on curtains, the ribbon and smells (and one can get carried away by food, I observed). And one should also appreciate the fact that this house was exceptionally "inner," and that this "inner-ness" manifested itself chiefly in window-stuffing and in the chipped saucer in which a small dried-out plaster of housefly poison had remained from the summer season.

Nevertheless, so that it could not be said that, in my pigheaded zeal to maintain a certain internal course, I neglected all other possibilities, I gave myself the trouble of checking whether there was really no passage from the servants' quarter to the masters' apartments except through the pantry, and I ascertained that there was not. I even went outside and, slowly, seemingly taking a stroll, walked all around the house on the melting snow. It was inconceivable that anyone could have got inside at night through the doors or through the windows which were protected with powerful shutters. Hence, if any deed were performed in this house at night, nobody could be suspect, except perhaps the valet Szczepan, who slept in the pantry. "Yes," I said sagaciously, "it was surely the valet Szczepan. No one but he, especially considering the baleful expression of his eyes."

Speaking thus, I pricked up my ears, for, through an open window pane, a voice reached me, but how different it was from that which I had heard only recently, how delightful, how promising, no longer the voice of a suffering queen, but rather a voice shaken by terror and anxiety, a trembling, weak, feminine voice, which, it seemed, gave me confidence, which tried to give me a helping hand. "Cecilia, Cecilia . . . look out the window. Has he gone? Take a look! Don't lean out, don't, he might see you. He might even come in here to spy; did you put away the linen? What is he looking for? What has he seen? Oh, my little Ignace! Oh God, why did he inspect that stove, what did he want with the dresser? Oh, it's terrible, all over the house. Never mind about me, let him do with me what he likes, but Tony, Tony won't stand it. To him this is blasphemy! He became dreadfully pale when I told him. Ah, I fear that his strength will give out."

If, however, the crime was of an inner character, as might be regarded as settled after the investigation (I continued to think), duty demanded that we admit that a murder committed by the valet with the likely purpose of robbery could under no circumstances be considered as one of an internal character. Suicide is something different; a man kills himself and everything happens inside; so is parricide, where, after all, one's own blood does the killing. As for the cockroach, the murderer must have destroyed it in the process.

Spinning such thoughts, I sat down in the study with a cigarette when Anthony came in. Seeing me he said "Hello," but somewhat more modestly than the first time; it even seemed to me that he was a little put out of countenance.

"You have a beautiful home," I said. "There is an unusually great serenity and cordiality here. A truly homey, warm home. Makes you think of childhood, of mother. Mother in her dressing gown, bitten-off fingernails, the want of a handkerchief. . . ."

"Home? Home, of course. . . . There are mice. But that's not. . . . Mother told me, you supposedly . . . that is. . . ."

"I know an excellent remedy against mice. Ratopex."

"Oh yes, I, I must absolutely go at them with more energy, more energy, much more energy. . . . They say that this morning you were in . . . Father's . . . that is rather . . . I am sorry . . . in the body's. . . ."

"Yes."

"Ah! And. . . ?"

"And? And what?"

"They say that you found . . . something?"

"Oh yes, I did. A dead cockroach."

"Dead cockroaches are also numerous here, that is cockroaches . . . I meant to say, cockroaches which are not dead."

"Did you love your father very much?" I asked, taking an album of pictures of Cracow from the table.

This question clearly surprised him. No, he had not been prepared for it; he cast his head down, looked aside, swallowed and said under his breath with unspeakable constraint, nearly with aversion.

"Pretty much. . . ."

"Pretty? That's not much. Pretty much! And with such aversion at that."

"Why do you ask?" he inquired in a muffled voice.

"Why are you so unnatural?" I replied in a tone of sympathy, leaning over to him in a fatherly manner, with the album in my hands.

"I? I, unnatural? How can. . . ?"

"Why did you turn white at this moment, white as a wall?"

"I? I turned white?"

"Oh, oh! You look round you furtively. . . . You don't
finish your sentences. . . . You speak of mice, cockroaches. . . . Your voice is too loud, then again too quiet,
hoarse, then again sort of shrill so that it pierces one's
eardrums," I spoke seriously. "And your gestures are so
nervous. Besides all of you are, how shall I say, nervous,
unnatural. Why is that, young man? Isn't it better to
mourn in a simple-minded way? Hm . . . 'pretty much'!
And why did you persuade your mother a week ago to
abandon your father's bedroom?"

Completely paralyzed by my words, not daring to move
an arm or a leg, he succeeded in uttering only:

"I? What do you mean? Father . . . Father . . . needed
. . . some fresh air. . . ."

"On the critical night you slept in your room downstairs?"

"I? In the room, of course . . . in the room downstairs."

I cleared my throat and went to my room, leaving him
on a chair, his hands folded on his knees, his mouth
tightly set and his legs stiffly joined together. "Hm, quite
probably, a nervous character. Nervous character, bashful
nature, excessive emotions, exaggerated cordiality. . . ."
But I still controlled myself, not wishing to frighten anyone or anything away. While I was washing my hands in
my room and getting ready for dinner, the valet Szczepan
slid into my room in order to ask whether I needed anything. He looked reborn; his eyes shot in all directions,
his demeanor revealed a cunning servility, and all his
spiritual forces were active to the highest degree. I asked:
"Well, what's new?"

He said in one breath: "That is, Your Honor, you asked
if whether I slept in the pantry the night before last.

I wanted to say that that night, in the evening, the young master locked the pantry door from the dining room." I asked: "Had the young master never locked that door?" "Never, absolutely never. Only that once and even so he probably thought I was asleep because it was late, but I was not yet asleep and I heard him go and lock it. When he unlocked it, I don't know, because I had fallen asleep; he woke me up in the morning to say that the old master was dead, and the door was unlocked then."

So for some unexplained reasons the dead man's son locks the pantry door at night! He locks the pantry door? What was this supposed to mean?

"Only, Your Honor, please do not say that I said anything."

It was not in vain that I designated the death as internal! The door was locked so that no stranger might have access to it. The net was tightening by the minute, the noose closing around the murderer's neck was becoming more and more discernible. Why then, instead of manifesting triumph, did I merely smile rather stupidly? Because—this must be admitted, alas—something was missing which was at least as important as the noose around the murderer's neck, namely, the noose around the victim's neck. Though I had skipped over that difficulty, though I had taken a naive leap over the neck, which sparkled with immaculate whiteness, one could not eternally stay in an absolving state of passion. All right, I agree (speaking off the record), I was angry; for one reason or another, hatred, disgust and insult had blinded me and made me maintain stubbornly such an obvious absurdity. That's only human, and everyone will understand. But the moment would come when I would have to calm down; as the Bible says, the day of Judgment will come. And then . . . hm . . . I would say: "Here is the murderer," and the corpse would say: "I died of a heart attack." And then what? What would the judgment be?

Let us suppose that the judge would ask: "You maintain that the man was murdered. On what basis?"

I should answer: "Because, Your Honor, his family, his wife and children, especially the son, are behaving ambiguously, they are behaving as though they had murdered him, there is no doubt."

"Good, but by what means could he be murdered, when he was not murdered, when the autopsy clearly demonstrates that he died simply of a heart attack?"

And then the attorney, that paid cheat, would rise and, in a long speech, waving the sleeves of his gown, he would begin to prove that there was a misunderstanding which originated in my low manner of reasoning; that I had confused crime and mourning, for what I took to express a guilty conscience was actually merely an expression of a modesty of feeling, which tends to shy away and to cringe under the cold touch of a stranger. And again the unbearable, boring refrain: "By what miracle was he murdered, since he has not been murdered at all, since there isn't the slightest trace of any strangling on the body?" would return.

This obstacle bothered me so that at the dinner table—just for myself, as it were, and in order to deafen my worry and to bring relief to the penetrating doubts, and without any other intention—I began to argue that, in its actual essence, crime was not physical, but rather psychological *par excellence.* If I am not mistaken, no one took the floor except myself. Anthony did not utter a word,

I don't know whether because he did not deem me worthy, as had been the case the previous night, or because he was afraid that his voice might sound a little hoarse. The widowed mother sat in her chair pontifically, continuing, I think, to feel mortally wounded, while her hands shook, seeking to assure themselves impunity. Cecilia silently swallowed liquids which were too hot. As for me, as a result of the internal motives mentioned above and realizing neither the tactlessness I was committing nor a certain tension in the atmosphere, I held forth volubly and at length.

"Believe me, ladies and gentleman, the physical form of a deed, the tortured body, disorder in the room and all the so-called traces, amount to nothing but a secondary detail, strictly speaking, nothing but an addition to the actual crime, a medical and judicial formality, the criminal's bow to the authorities and nothing else. The actual crime is always carried out in the soul. External details . . . good God! I will cite the following case. A young man suddenly, and without explanation, pushes a long, old-fashioned hatpin into the back of his uncle and benefactor, who has heaped favors upon him for thirty years. There you are. Such a great psychological crime and such a small, almost invisible, physical trace, a tiny hole in the back caused by the sting of a pin. The nephew later explained that he had absent-mindedly taken his uncle's back for his cousin's hat. But who would believe him?

"Oh yes, physically speaking, crime is a trifle; it is difficult only spiritually. Because of the extraordinary frailty of the human organism, one can commit a murder by accident or, like that nephew, by absent-mindedness, and out of nowhere, suddenly, bang, there's the corpse.

"A certain woman, the kindest woman in the world and madly in love with her husband, at the height of their honeymoon, noticed a longish worm crawling in the raspberries on her husband's plate, and I must tell you that her husband hated those hideous worms more than anything. Instead of warning him, she watched him with a flirtatious smile and then said: 'You have eaten a worm!' 'No,' the terrified husband cries. 'But you have,' the wife answers and she describes it: 'it was such and such, fat and white.' There was much laughter and teasing; the man, pretending to be cross, flung his arms up to heaven, bemoaning his wife's malice. The whole thing was forgotten. A week or two later the woman was greatly astonished to see her husband lose weight, dry up, return all food; disgusted with his own arms and legs, he (forgive the expression) did not stop vomiting. His disgust towards himself increased, turning into a terrible illness! And then one day: terrible tears, awful moans, for he died suddenly, having thrown himself up so thoroughly into the bucket that only his head and throat remained. The widow was in despair. Finally, it came out in the severe cross-examination that, in the most remote corners of her consciousness, she felt an unnatural attraction towards a bulldog which her husband had beaten shortly before eating the raspberries.

"Or another case. In an aristocratic family a young man murdered his mother by continuously repeating the irritating word: 'terrific!' In court he pretended to be innocent to the end. Oh, crime is such an easy thing that you wonder how come so many people die a natural death . . . especially when the heart, the heart becomes entangled in it, that mysterious link among men, that intricate underground corridor between you and me, that suction and force pump, which can suck so excellently and force so marvelously. Afterwards an atmosphere of mourning prevails, graveyard faces, the dignity of suffering, the majesty of death, ha, ha, and all that for the purpose of having suffering 'respected' and so that nobody might look more closely into that heart which imperceptibly committed a cruel murder!"

They sat there like church mice, not daring to interrupt me. Where was yesterday's pride? Suddenly the widow threw her napkin down and, as pale as death, her hands trembling twice as fast as usual, rose from the table. I spread my hands. "I am very sorry. I didn't mean to hurt anyone. I was just speaking generally about the heart, the cardiac sack, in which a corpse may be hidden so easily."

"Villain!" she uttered, her breast heaving heavily. Her son and daughter jumped from the table.

"The door!" I cried out. "All right, 'villain.' But could someone tell me why the door was locked last night?"

A pause. All of a sudden Cecilia broke into nervous moaning, weeping, and, sobbing, she said:

"The door, it wasn't Mother. I locked it. I did!"

"That's not true, my daughter. I ordered the door locked. Why do you humble yourself before this man?"

"You ordered it, Mother, but I wanted to . . . I wanted . . . I also wanted to lock the door and I locked it."

"Excuse me," I said, "just a moment. How's this (I knew that Anthony had locked the pantry door)? Which door are you talking about?"

"The door . . . the door of Daddy's bedroom. I locked it!"

"It was I who locked it. I forbid you to speak like this, do you hear? I had it locked!"

What was this? So they, too, had locked doors? The night the father was to die, his son locked the pantry door, while mother and daughter locked the door of their room!

"And why did you, ladies, lock that door," I asked impetuously, "exceptionally, particularly on that night? For what purpose?"

Consternation! Silence! They did not know! They bowed their heads! A theatrical scene. Then Anthony's agitated voice resounded.

"Aren't you ashamed to explain? And to whom? Keep quiet! Let us go!"

"Ah! In that case maybe you can tell me why you locked the pantry door that night, thus keeping the servants away from the other rooms?"

"I? I locked the door?"

"Well? Perhaps you didn't? There are witnesses. This can be proved."

Silence again! Consternation again! The women stared into space with terror. Finally the son, as though recalling something from long ago, declared in a dull voice:

"I did."

"But why? Why did you lock the door? Perhaps because of drafts?"

"This I cannot explain," he replied with a haughtiness which would be difficult to describe, and he left the room.

I spent the rest of the day in my room. Without lighting the candle I paced up and down from wall to wall for a long while. Outside nightfall thickened; the snow patches stood out with increasing vividness in the falling shadow of the night, and the entangled skeletons of trees surrounded the house from all sides.

Here's a house for you! A house of murderers, a monstrous house, where cold-blooded, well concealed, premeditated murder prevails! A house of stranglers! The heart? Right away I knew what to expect of that well fed heart and what kind of parricide this heart had had, this heart stuffed with fat, nurtured with butter and family warmth. I knew it, but I didn't want to say anything prematurely! And they were so proud! They demanded such homage! Feeling? They had better tell why they locked the doors!

Why then, at the moment when I held all the threads in my hand and could point a finger at the murderer, why did I waste my time instead of acting? That obstacle, that one obstacle—that white, untouched neck which, like the snow outside, became the whiter, as the nightfall darkened. The corpse must have taken part in the plot of the murderous gang. I made an effort once more and approached the corpse in a frontal attack this time, with the visor down, calling a spade a spade and clearly pointing at the wrongdoer. But it was like fighting a chair. No matter how I strained my imagination, my intuition and logic, the neck remained a neck, whiteness was still whiteness, with the characteristic stubbornness of inanimate objects. There was therefore nothing left to do but to hold out to the end, to insist on the vengeful fallacy and absurdity and to wait, to wait, counting naively on the possibility that, if the corpse was not willing, maybe, maybe the truth would float to the surface on its own—like oil. Was I wasting my time? Yes, but my strides resounded in the house, and everyone could hear that I was walking ceaselessly, and they were probably not idle downstairs.

Dinner time had passed. Eleven o'clock approached, but I still had not moved from the room, continuing to call them such names as scoundrels and murderers. I triumphed, while, at the same time, hoping with the rest of my strength that stubbornness and perseverance would be rewarded, that such passion would soften the heart of the situation after so many endeavors, so many different facial expressions, that it would finally not be able to resist and that, tense, led to the summit of its patience, it would have to resolve itself somehow, to give birth to something, to something no longer in the realm of fiction, but something real. For we could not go on like this forever: I—upstairs, they—downstairs; somebody had to say: "I pass," but everything depended on who would do it first. All was tranquil and noiseless. I peered out into the hall, but no sound came from downstairs. What could they be doing down there? Were they at least doing what was expected of them? While I triumphed up here because of all those locked doors, were they, on their part, sufficiently frightened, were they deliberating adequately, straining their ears, groping for the sound of my footsteps, or were their souls too lazy to work all this out? "Ah," I sighed with relief when at about midnight I at last heard footsteps in the hall and someone knocked at my door. "Come in," I cried.

"I am sorry," Anthony said, sitting down in a chair which I pointed out to him. He looked unhealthy, pale and ashen; I could tell that coherent speech would not be his strongest point. "Your behavior . . . and then those words . . . in other words, what is all this supposed to mean? Either leave our house immediately . . . or tell me! This is blackmail!" he burst out.

"So you finally asked me," I said. "Rather late! And even now you speak in very general terms. What should I say, I wonder. But all right. Well, your father has been. . . ."

"What? What has he been?"

"Strangled."

"Strangled. All right. Strangled." He shuddered with a kind of strange pleasure.

"Are you glad?"

"I am."

I waited a moment and then said:

"Had you any other questions?"

He burst out:

"But nobody heard any screams, any noise."

"First of all, only your mother and sister slept nearby and they had shut their door tight for the night. Secondly, the murderer could have choked the victim at once, and. . . ."

"All right, all right," he whispered, "all right. One moment. One more question. This is it. Who, according to you . . . whom do you. . . ."

"Suspect. Isn't that right? Whom do I suspect? What do you think? Would you say that during the night someone from the outside could get into a house so tightly closed, guarded by a watchman and vigilant dogs? You will probably say that the dogs had fallen asleep along with the watchman, and the entrance door had by mistake been left open? Is that right? What an unfortunate coincidence!"

"No one could have entered," he replied proudly. He sat very straight, and one could see that, in his immobility, he despised me with all his heart.

"No one," I eagerly confirmed, joyously anticipating seeing his pride. "Absolutely no one! So the persons left are the three of you and three servants. But the servants' access was cut off because you, God knows why, locked the pantry door. Perhaps you will now claim that you did not lock it?"

"I locked it!"

"But why, for what purpose did you lock it?"

He jumped from his chair. "Don't put on airs!" I said and with this brief remark I grounded him on the chair. His anger died down, as if paralyzed, breaking off on a squeeky note.

"I locked it, I don't know, automatically," he said with difficulty and he whispered twice: "Choked to death, choked to death." Nervous nature! They all had a deep, nervous nature!

"And because your mother and sister also . . . automatically locked their bedroom door—besides, it would be difficult to suppose, wouldn't it?—there is left . . . you know who is left. Only you had free access to your father that night. 'The plowman homeward plods his weary way, And leaves the world to darkness and to me.' "

He burst out:

"Is this perhaps supposed to mean that . . . that I . . . Ha, ha, ha!"

"And this laughter is perhaps supposed to mean that it wasn't you," I observed, and his laughter, after a few attempts, died out on a protracted, false note.

"Not you? In that case, young man," I began more softly, "will you explain to me why you did not shed a single tear?"

"A tear?"

"Yes, a tear. This is what your mother confessed to me in a whisper, oh, right at the beginning, yesterday on the stairs. It is usual for mothers to disgrace and betray their children. And now a little while ago you laughed. You declared that you were glad of your father's death," I said with triumphant obtuseness, pouncing on his words until, his strength failing, he looked at me as if I were a blind instrument of torture.

Yet sensing the increasing gravity of the situation, gathering all his will power, he attempted to stoop to an explanation in the form of an *avis au lecteur,* an aside, as it were, which barely came out of his throat.

"This was . . . sarcasm . . . you understand? . . . The other way round . . . on purpose."

"Being sarcastic about your father's death?"

He was silent, and then I whispered confidentially, almost straight into his ear.

"Why are you so embarrassed? After all, a father's death . . . there's nothing embarrassing about that."

As I recall that moment, I am glad that I got out of it safely, though he did not even move.

"Perhaps you are embarrassed because you loved him? Perhaps you really loved him?"

He stammered with difficulty, with disgust, with despair:

"All right. If you insist . . . if . . . then, yes, all right . . . I did."

And throwing something on the table, he cried out:

"Look! It's his hair."

It was indeed a tuft of hair. "All right," I said, "take it away."

"I don't want to! You can take it. I give it to you."

"What are all these outbursts for? All right, you loved

him, that's fine. Only one more question—because, as you see, I don't understand much about those romances of yours. I admit, you have almost succeeded in convincing me with this tuft of hair, but, you see, there's mainly one thing I don't grasp."

Here I lowered my voice again and whispered into his ear.

"You loved him, that's all right, but why is there so much embarrassment, so much disdain in that love?"

He turned white and said nothing.

"So much cruelty and disgust? Why do you hide your love, the way a murderer hides his murder. You don't answer? You don't know? Perhaps I will know for you. You loved him. You did, but when your father got ill . . . you tell your mother about the need for fresh air. Your mother, who, by the way, loved him too, listens and nods. True, true, fresh air cannot do any harm; so she moves to her daughter's room, thinking: 'I will be close to him and ready for the sick man's call.' Was it not so? Would you correct me?"

"It was so."

"Exactly! I am an old bird, you see. A week passes by. One evening mother and daughter lock their bedroom. Why? Only God knows. Is it essential to ponder over every turning of the key in a lock? One, two, three, they turned it, automatically, and jumped into bed. Yes, and simultaneously you lock the pantry door downstairs. One might as well demand an explanation of the fact that you are at present sitting rather than standing."

He jumped to his feet, then sat down again and said:

"Yes, that's the way it was. It was exactly as you say!"

"And then it occurs to you that your father might still need something. Perhaps, you are thinking, Mother and Sister have both fallen asleep and Father needs something. And so, noiselessly, you go up on the creaking stairs to your father's room. Well and when you found yourself in the room—the remainder requires no comment—you automatically went all the way."

He listened without believing his ears, but suddenly he seemed to start and he groaned with a kind of desperate frankness which can be inspired only by great fear.

"But I had not been up there at all! I spent the whole night in my room downstairs. I not only locked the pantry door, but I also locked myself in. I also locked myself in my room. . . . There must be a mistake!"

I exclaimed:

"What? You, too, locked yourself in? It seems that everybody did. Then who was it?"

"I don't know, I don't know," he replied with astonishment, rubbing his forehead. "Only now do I begin to understand that we may have expected something; we may have had presentiments, and, for fear and shame," he burst out violently, "everybody turned his key . . . because we would have wished Father, Father . . . to attend to this business alone."

"Ah, I see, sensing that death was approaching, you locked yourselves in before the oncoming death? So you did await that murder?"

"We awaited it?"

"Yes. But in that case who murdered him? Because he *was* murdered, while you only waited, and no stranger could have possibly got in."

He was silent.

"But I tell you, I was really in my room, locked in," he whispered at last, bending under the weight of unanswerable logic. "There is a mistake."

"But in that case, who murdered him?" I said laboriously. "Who murdered him?"

He pondered, as though drawing a terrible account of his conscience and weighing his innermost intentions. He was pale, his glance, under his lowered eyelids, backed away inside. Did he notice something there in his own depth? What did he notice? Did he perhaps see himself rising from the bed and carefully stepping on the treacherous stairs, his hands ready for action? Maybe for a mere moment he was overtaken by the uncertain thought that after all, who knows, such a thing would not be absolutely out of the question. Perhaps in this one second hatred appeared to him as a complement of love, who knows (this is only my supposition) whether in this fraction of an instant he did not come upon the terrible duality of all feeling, in which love and hatred are two facets of one feeling. This blinding though passing revelation (such, at least, is my interpretation) must have wreaked havoc on everything within him so that, wrapped up in this love of his, he became unbearable to himself. And although this lasted only a moment, it was enough. After all, he had been forced to fight against my suspicion for twelve hours already; for twelve hours he had felt a senseless and stubborn pursuit behind him and he must have digested the absurdity of the thought a thousand times. Like a broken man, he bent his head and then he said distinctly straight into my face:

"I did. I . . . went."

"What do you mean by 'went'?"

"I went, I said, I went ahead, as you said, automatically, all the way."

"What? It's true! You admit it? It was you? You, really and truly?"

"I. I went."

"Ah, that's it. And the whole thing took no more than a minute."

"No more. A minute at most. We may even be overestimating it. A minute. And then I returned to my room, lay down and fell asleep, and before I fell asleep I yawned and I thought, I remember this well, that, oh, oh, tomorrow I would have to get up in the morning!"

I was dumbfounded; his whole confession was so smooth, perhaps not quite so smooth (for his voice became hoarse) as rabid, filled with extraordinary delight. There was no doubting it! There was no denying it! All right, but the neck, what could be done with the neck which obtusely maintained its own claim in the bedroom? My mind worked feverishly, but what could a mind do against a dead man's mindlessness?

Depressed, I glanced at the murderer who seemed to wait. And—it is difficut to explain—at that moment I realized that there was nothing left for me to do but to make a frank admission. Knocking my head against the wall, that is, against the neck, was useless, any further resistance or machinations, hopeless. As soon as I had realized this, I developed great trust in him. I realized that I had pushed too far, that I had done a trifle too much mischief, and, in my trouble, exhausted and out of breath after so many efforts and facial effects, I suddenly became a child, a small helpless boy who wished to confess his mistake and prank to his elder brother. It seemed to me that he would understand and would not refuse me his advice. "Yes," I thought, "that's all that's left: a frank confession. He will understand, he will help! He will find a way out!" But, just in case, I got up and gradually went closer to the door.

"You see," I said, and my lips shook a little, "there is a certain difficulty . . . a certain obstacle, a formalistic one, to be sure, nothing important. The thing is that," I touched the doorknob, " that, to tell the truth, the body does not reveal any traces of strangling. Physiologically speaking, he was not choked to death at all, but died normally of a heart attack. The neck, you know, the neck! The neck is untouched!"

Having said this, I dived into the half-open door and ran along the hall as fast as I could. I burst into the room where the body lay and hid in the wardrobe. With great hopefulness, though with fear, I waited. The space was dark, close and sultry, and the dead man's trousers rubbed against my cheek. I waited a long time and began to doubt; I thought that nothing would happen, that they had basely made a fool of me and tricked me. The door opened quietly, and someone slid cautiously inside. Then I heard a dreadful noise. The bed creaked like mad in the perfect silence; all the formalities were being attended to *ex post facto*. Then the footsteps withdrew just as they had come. When, after a lengthy hour, trembling and perspiring, I got out of the wardrobe, violence and force prevailed in the messy bed linen; the body had been thrown diagonally across the creased pillow, and the corpse's neck revealed the distinct impression of all the ten fingers. Although the medical experts were not quite pleased with those fingerprints (they said that there was something about them that was not quite as it should be), the fingerprints, together with the murderer's clear confession at the trial, were finally considered as adequate legal basis.

JÓZEF MACKIEWICZ (1903(?)–   ) is now living in Western Germany, where he is preparing a collection of his short stories and working on a new novel. Journalist, editor, novelist, playwright, historian and literary critic, he has, moreover, led an active life as a soldier and patriot. His creative work deserves to be more widely presented in English.

BRONISLAS DE LEVAL JEZIERSKI, the translator, is a Bostonian and a lecturer on Slavic languages and literatures at Tufts University.

The Adventures of an Imp

JÓZEF MACKIEWICZ

$\mathcal{T}$he kitchen stove was already completely cold when Little Nick came home from school. His mother was just pinning on her bat's wings, evidently planning to go out.

"I want to eat," he said.

"Look around for yourself—there may be something left yet—but don't bother me, I'm in a hurry."

"I want to eat!"

"Tell that to Daddy when he comes back," she answered with a spiteful tone in her voice.

Mrs. Devil really was in a hurry and, taking a short cut, flew out the window, closing it behind her. But a moment later she was back knocking at the vent.

"Hand me my pitchfork."

"Where is it?" he answered sulkily.

"You always have a thousand and one questions! Look for it!"

She hovered in space, playing nervously with the hook of the vent. Little Nick found the pitchfork in the corner of the hallway and poked it through the vent.

"One never hands things to anyone with the sharp end pointing out!" she rebuked him and flew off.

The imp was attending the lowest grade of grammar school, and his parents were not faring too well. He gulped something down quickly, expecting his daddy to come home hungry also.

After a little less than an hour had passed, his father came in, tired and gloomy. He worked at the cauldrons and was smeared all over with pitch to which remnants of the good deeds of sinful souls still clung.

"Get this filth off me," he said with disgust, for he could not stand physical labor, least of all on the very lowest rung of the diabolical proletariat.

He was always full of aspirations and considered himself an intellectual. He was, however, unable to cope with life, hence was forced to a job of menial labor.

"Where's Mama?" he asked, shaking off some of the scum.

"She's flown off somewheres."

"The angels must have given me such a housekeeper!" he swore, kicking fitfully at a stool and sighing deeply at the same time.

He sat down near the window and unfolded the latest issue of *The Diabolical Courier,* the organ of the moderate center. For even though he was a workingman, he never read the radical *Satanic Gazette,* since he did not approve of its demagogic and shrill tone. On this day, however, all the papers, regardless of their orientation, even down to the clerical-conservative organ, *Dale of Demons,* were full of similar-sounding messages regarding a border dispute: "Celestial Imperialism," "We Will Not Surrender What Is Ours," "There Is Not a Devil in Hell, or in the Universe, Who Would Consent . . . ," "Provocative Behavior of the Angelic Guards," etc. These were the type of headlines appearing on the front pages of the press. The matter in question concerned a trifling border incident at the point where Hell touched on Purgatory.

The devil yawned and stretched out his hooves.

"Daddy," said Little Nick, "I'm going out to play a bit."

"It seems that you never do anything else," answered a voice from behind the newspaper. "Have you prepared tomorrow's lesson?"

"Well. . . ."

"What did you study today?"

"How to persuade human children to play with matches and to filch sweets from the pantry."

The father yawned again and glanced at the window. Beyond it he could see foggy smoke, reddened by the glare of burning tar. He pushed open the window and looked out. Twilight was just descending on Earth. The unpleasant sound of bells mingled with the snarl of airplane propellers and automobile horns. Little Nick, too, ran up to the window, and, resting with one hand against his father's shoulder, leaned out quite far over the sill. They watched for a while in silence. Everything could be seen quite close, so that the father spat and aimed right into the chimney of the Simon Bros. and Co. factory, which turned out raincoats. You could also see things from their astronomical perspective. You did not even have to blink an eye; you merely had to wish. For some time, Little Nick amused himself childishly with this innate ability; then he suddenly asked:

"Is the Earth below?"

"There is no below or above."

"Then where is Heaven?"

"On the other side."

"On what side?"

"A different one."

The little imp, hanging over the ledge, kicked against the wall with his little hooves, spat, but hit nothing.

"Well then, what is our Hell?"

"It is a point of view enclosed in a circle."

"And Heaven?"

"Another point of view enclosed in another circle."

"I don't understand."

"There are a lot of things you don't understand yet. You will understand them when you go to college instead of to elementary school. In the meanwhile, don't bother me."

"No! Tell me, Daddy!"

"What do you want? Go do your lessons for tomorrow!"

"And is that how it will be forever?"

"Forever."

"And what will happen when Forever ends?"

"Hush! Nobody knows that."

The father looked around and then whispered:

"Perhaps there will come a terrible cataclysm which will destroy the points of view. Then will come the ruin of us all, both Hell and Heaven."

"But who will be able to do this?"

"I don't know, son, but there were once some very learned devils who claimed that Truth will do this, after the end of Eternity. But the court sentenced them to three hundred billion years of hard labor, as well as to deprivation of fire and to the amputation of their horns. Don't even think about such things."

"But couldn't Hell make an agreement with Heaven, so the two of them could fight Truth together?"

At this moment the door slammed.

"Go on, go on, teach your child blasphemies," shrieked the mother from the threshold. "He's already running around with delinquents! Just now a neighbor was telling me how he and some street urchins were handing water to parched, flaming souls. A fine state of affairs! Do you want him to grow up to be a bandit?"

Hereupon she lifted Little Nick's tail and gave him a few well-felt whacks.

He ran out sobbing, but consoled himself with the fact that they hadn't made him do his lessons. The little devils of the neighborhood were just discussing going to the moon. Little Nick had already gone on several such expeditions. His namesake, Old Nick, lived there in his own palace. The whole point of the game was to hide behind a rock and call out: "Peek-a-Boo!" which threw the old devil into a fit of rage; after this one had to run for one's life. The imp might even have gone this time too, except that just at this moment a resplendent carriage, drawn by eight fiery steeds, rolled through the main street of the little town. The inhabitants poured out into the open. Some, especially those who were not members of trade unions, bowed low. In the carriage sat Mephistopheles, delegated to take personal part in the parley to solve the border conflict. Little Nick broke into a run, reached the carriage and, after the fashion of street arabs, clambered on the rear axle and hung onto the springs with his hands.

The road went slightly uphill. Just beyond the little town they had to detour around a group of recently damned who were being led in a convoy. The stragglers were being prodded with forks. Their tears turned into hail about the size of cobblestones, and the carriage began to lurch fearfully. Mephistopheles liked a swift ride. He once had heard an anecdote about an imperial courier, sent by Prince Potemkin with a missive to Catherine II, who traveled with such speed that the end of his sword, hanging by accident out of the carriage, rattled against the mileposts as if they were a picket fence. Mephistopheles would deliberately hang out his sword and ask to be driven so fast that it would clatter against the mileposts. For the last hundred years, however, he had been suffering from sciatica on his right side; so, hissing with pain, he rapped at the front window:

"I say, diavolo, isn't there some way around all this?"

"No, there is not, Your Honor, but we turn left soon. Purgatory is not far off."

"Then slow down a bit."

The driver reluctantly pulled in the reins, and the steeds ambled along, much to Little Nick's disappointment.

Upon arriving at the frontier Mephistopheles was assisted in alighting by two flunkies. He looked around with distaste. He loathed the countryside, disorder, the barking of dogs and broad vistas. Nearby was encamped a detachment of devils armed with flame-throwers. Opposite them paced an angel with a wide, squarish face and blond hair in a crew cut. From the stubborn set of his mouth and his somewhat vacant expression, he could be recognized as a man of the people. Purgatory guards were largely chosen from such as he. Across his wings he had slung an automatic pistol which ejected holy water. His arms, with the sleeves rolled up to the elbow, were like rocks. Mephistopheles, who would willingly have conceded several billion square miles just so as not to be marooned in these sticks, rubbed his side and turned to the sergeant of his detachment:

"What is this wretched place called?"

"Devil's Gulch, Your Honor," answered the latter, stiffening to attention.

"All right! And where is their plenipotentiary?" he inquired, motioning over his shoulder with his thumb at the angel.

"They've signaled that he is on his way in his chariot. At least that's what they say. . . . But they. . . ."

"Well, good enough, good enough."

Little Nick expected more interesting things. The angel pacing the clouds seemed to be scrutinizing his big toe which was sticking out of his sandal. It was a sight worth seeing! Such a way for a leg to end seemed hilarious to Little Nick. He crawled out from under the carriage and climbed onto a cloud in order to see better.

"Scat!" an angel cried out to him.

Little Nick climbed down and approached the diabolical sergeant.

"Then there won't be a war?" he asked in a soft descant.

"Whoever wants one!" rejoined the old timer.

"How about them?" he asked, pointing to the angelic defenses dug into the clouds.

"Why would they want a war?" The sergeant suddenly came to: "What are you hanging around here for? I've had enough of you! Take off!"

Little Nick ran away. Night fell. Misty exhalations and smoky columns now became motionless. Above the furnaces the clouds gathered, multi-storied, decorative, red, delicately shaping into black ravens, cats and bats.

Lucifer's ancient carriage, hurled down in its day from the Milky Way, lay neglected, as it had for a long time, without wheels and without future. But it was not sight, but the sense of hearing that revealed the most characteristic traits of the surroundings. Everywhere there was a whizzing and a great howling. A howling in honor of the night and of evil, for such was the eternal attitude toward things. At times the howling became so strong that it even deadened the groans of the tortured souls. However, when it fell off in strength one could hear from afar, from the skyscraping distance, the evening chorales of the angels singing the hymn to justice being fulfilled.

One could smell brimstone, smoke and tar. Actually there was once a time when they had begun to install piping for oil-heating, but before the first refinery had been finished there arose the project of condensing lightning. Lucifer had approved this project, when from Earth came the news about the discovery of atomic energy. One couldn't keep up. The *Satanic Gazette* ran a malicious notice to the effect that, if things continued this way, Earth would become a Hell more exemplary than Hell itself. Lucifer sentenced the editor to one hundred years in a barrel of holy water, but even this draconian punishment did not succeed in preventing further talk about reaction and backward conditions. In the meanwhile, one continued, as of old, to burn tar.

To Little Nick, who for the first time had seen its confines, Hell suddenly seemed small, boring and oppressive, but especially monotonous. At home he found "Heaven itself," as his father would brutally announce. His mother had already had too much of all this. She made tremendous scenes and brought all the blame to bear upon the ineptitude of her spouse.

"Everybody," she would say, "gets along somehow! Everyone can obtain some sort of diabolical post, but you are stuck in this tar. You come home and read the paper! Instead of thinking, going to the devil, talking things over, making inquiries, making some sort of effort!"

"Do it yourself," he answered lackadaisically. This led her to near madness.

For in fact she had tried and knew that it was getting more difficult every day. All the jobs on earth were already taken. The distinguished Beelzebub clan had preempted the best ones for themselves. The head of the family, Beelzebub the Genial, with whom even Lucifer himself had to remain on good terms, held the most profitable post, under Stalin's skin. Lesser relatives had all become so high and mighty that without their protection it was utterly impossible to obtain a position in any civilized family worthy of the name. Just recently the employment office had proposed that Mrs. D. take a job among the . . . Pygmies! In the African Congo! And this in all earnest. The secretary at the employment office had shifted on her chair—she had accidentally sat on her own tail—put on her spectacles, and reached for the geographical atlas. In answer to this, Mrs. D. had slammed the door as she stormed out. Now she repeated the proposition to her husband with a sort of malicious satisfaction.

"You can crawl over tree tops yourself if you care to," he answered. "I have no intention either to break my legs or to pick up malaria. One can become a savage chasing after any old gorilla."

"What sort of nonsense is that? Gorillas don't have souls."

"Whether they do or not, I don't consider the Pygmies on a much higher level."

"Why, you've never even seen one."

"I can assure you that I have not the slightest desire to."

Little Nick's entry interrupted the discussion. His mother had to upbraid him for loafing about, no one even knew where. His father seized this opportunity to reach for the evening edition of the *Courier* and to lose himself in "Earthly Affairs." For a long time a bitter polemic had raged over this subject. The radical *Satanic Gazette* sharply attacked the infernal delegates who stood behind the chairs of the UN Assembly for their inability to incline the members sufficiently toward peace. "If the warmongers," complained the special correspondent, "succeed in bringing about a war with the Soviet Union, they are in a position to nullify our work and to diminish considerably the biological basis of our position on earth." The *Courier* held a completely opposite point of view, and maintained that Soviet diplomacy had led to results which contradicted the aims of Hell. "Millions of humans in concentration camps are undergoing a sort of Hell on Earth, and in this way, purging themselves through suffering, they attain Heaven when they die. This state of affairs must be stopped." The article ended with a discreet allusion to the Beelzebub clan whose personal gains overshadowed the public interests of Hell. The clerical-conservative *Dale of Demons*, which notoriously insisted on every *status quo* and did not like war, upheld the radical position: "Political realism," it said, "teaches us that peo-

ple in concentration camps, regardless of what they suf-
fer, become worse and not better. Whence does the
Courier draw its statistics about the influx to Heaven in
recent times? These figures do not seem convincing to us.
We have been carrying on a cold war with Heaven for in-
numerable astronomical years, and the state of co-exist-
ence does not damage our interests, which could, however,
be seriously jeopardized by an opportunistic war whose
very outcome is doubtful. Similarly on Earth, a war with
the Soviet Union would endanger our holdings there. We
must above all be on the alert against the interference of
foreign agents in our straightforward political line."

Little Nick's father felt that all of these views did not
and never could change the basic state of affairs and
secretly agreed with his wife that mulling over them was
a waste of time. He turned the page and, running his
eyes over the classified advertisements, suddenly jumped
up, recalling that today he was working the night-shift.
He threw the paper down onto the chair, placed his foot
on it, and rapidly began brushing his hoof. At precisely
this moment his glance fell on an ad in the "Help Wanted"
section:

"Wanted at once a small imp for a good family on
Earth. Scrupulous guardianship assured. Light duties. Apply to . . . ," he didn't finish reading. It was late.

"Look," he only said to his wife as he seized his fork
and went out.

Ten minutes later the mother, having changed her
son's clothes, flew with him to the designated address.
They were received by a devil, no longer young, but still
in his prime, dignified, with poised gestures. With two
fingers he lifted Little Nick's chin and smiled. The little

199

devil pleased him. He walked about the room as he spoke and rubbed his hands together with a certain unctuousness. He had come here from Earth on a three-day leave in order to attend to certain pressing family matters. He had an excellent position with the quiet family of a manufacturer of dried fruits in a large European city. They were very solid people, well-to-do, young. He had been having a little trouble, however, as the three children began to grow up. After all, he couldn't strain himself—and he made a helpless gesture with his hands.

"Moreover," he continued, "childish affairs have long since evaporated from my brain. I would, therefore, like a small assistant. Think you can manage?" he asked, turning to Little Nick. "Well?"

The latter stood shyly and did not answer.

"He's always like that, but only at first," hastily explained the mother, pulling her son unobtrusively by the tail. "He livens up later."

"That's a minor matter. I won't be too exacting. At first it will be a question of only the most elementary duties. He must see to it that the children eventually quarrel among themselves and occasionally get into a fight. But now that's not important. As I say, I will be easy on him. Let them just play once in a while with their father's razor blade, turn on the gas in the kitchen, or the water in the bathroom."

"So there is running water?" asked Mrs. D. with interest.

"But of course! Anyway, my dear lady, it is a matter of trifles, insignificant things, I don't even know. . . ."

"He's gone through all that at school."

"So much the better, so much the better! In that case

we can fly off together tomorrow. I am not one of those hoof-lickers who kill themselves in the service. People say: 'The hasty way is the devil's way.' Naturally they don't know what they are prating. A devil should always act with deliberation and prudence. At any rate, I will have time to instruct the little one a bit, since I also have a Wench whom I send where I myself am of no use."

"But perhaps she is one of those," interrupted the mother somewhat disturbed, "who are capable of depraving even . . . ?"

"You can rest easy on that score. This is a very solid person."

Mrs. D., who had never openly displayed any maternal sentiment for her son, felt, now that she had to, that it was really not so easy. Despite the fact that since her adversities she entertained a dislike for well-situated devils, she nonetheless was still pleased at placing Little Nick into what are called reliable hands. So she only sighed and thanked him.

II

The manufacturer's house consisted of many rooms. They arrived at midnight, gaining access through the large mirror in the parlor. Little Nick wanted to examine the many interesting objects, but the journey and the experiences he had undergone made him drowsy. He first saw the children the next day. There were two boys and one girl. He bashfully whispered to them that they should dawdle over dressing, but nobody heard him. It was a bright morning and the sunlight flooded the room when the chambermaid drew open the curtains.

"Untie her apron from behind," Little Nick whispered to little Peter, the eldest child, but the latter ran to the bathroom.

He therefore skipped over to the girl's bedroom; the chambermaid was just wishing her "Good-morning."

"Did the little Miss sleep well?"

"Tell her it's none of her business!" he said, thinking at the same time: "What silly advice!"

"Thank you. I had a lovely dream."

Little Nick became very anxious and ashamed of himself. Most of all he felt that his temptations were inept. Yet all this pleased him immensely and he very much wanted to stay. "What will happen," he thought, "if I turn out to be a failure?"

At breakfast he almost had tears in his eyes from exasperation and from fear lest the Chief walk in at any minute to check on his abilities. He began to plead with the children to misbehave at least a little bit, but they simply paid no attention to him. He therefore sat down on the red-hot coals in the fireplace and looked on as the girl, playing at being mother, fed her doll with a little silver spoon. "How nice it would be," he mused, "if the Chief came in, and here the boy would have already broken the clock on the mantelpiece; if the other boy had torn the doll away from his sister and smashed it against the floor, and if she had kicked him in the belly and had grabbed the corner of the tablecloth and pulled down the china. And the Chief would then say: 'Well, Little Nick, I see you are quite a lad after all!' Ah! childish dreams!"

"Well, Little Nick," said the Devil, parting the flames in the fireplace and entering the dining-room, "don't be downcast. Every beginning is difficult. When you get to know humans better you will learn how hard it is to persuade them to do evil. Our adversary, the Guardian Angel, has exactly the same difficulty in persuading them to do good. People just want to stick to their old points of view. Well, horns up!"

Little Nick wiped the tears from his cheeks with the back of his hand.

"But how should one go about it?" he asked meekly.

"Practice will show you. I don't know if you will understand this from the very start, but the greatest hindrance is the fact that humans, by their very nature, are fond of colors and even various shades of the same color. Our ideal, on the other hand, is that they see everything in one color—black, just as the ideal of our opposite numbers from Heaven is that everything be seen as white. Half of the work will be done as soon as the human soul is transformed from multicolor to . . . how shall I phrase it? . . . to, well, let us say, black and white stripes."

"Like a zebra, then?" exclaimed Little Nick who didn't really understand but immediately cheered up.

At this moment the Angel entered the room. He stroked the children's heads fondly and, with restrained dignity, but still politely, nodded in the Chief's direction.

"Get up and make a nice bow," whispered the Chief to Little Nick. "Remember to be always polite. Coarseness of manners has more than once caused us harm."

The Angel smiled fleetingly, nodded back, and entered the matrimonial bed-chamber.

"But sir!" stammered Little Nick. "Sir, aren't you afraid to let him go in alone like that? Isn't he likely to play some dirty trick?"

"One doesn't say 'dirty trick,' but 'cross our plans.'

Angels always 'cross.' Besides, I have the Wench for matrimonial matters."

The little imp saw her only after quite some time had elapsed. In his simplicity he had thought that the Wench would look like some of the witches he had seen in Hell. She turned out to be slender and beautiful. She had light hair, elongated heavenly-blue eyes, and Little Nick at once became convinced that this was after all not such a bad color. She had long eye-lashes, heavily painted, to be sure. First of all she embraced and kissed the lady of the house, then the children one after the other, leaving traces of lipstick on their cheeks. Next she said many pleasant things to everyone. "This must be some sort of misunderstanding," thought Little Nick. She crossed one pretty leg over the other pretty leg, and, from the divan where he was sitting, he could see under her skirt a rounded thigh and the fringe of her panties.

The Devil came in, whispered something in her ear, and she turned her blonde head and became still more affable to the wife of the manufacturer.

"I don't understand," sighed Little Nick and turned to the children.

Recently he had at last managed to get them to quarrel a few times. Peter, the oldest, moreover, once had almost set fire to the curtains, while the younger had poured a few drops of gasoline into the holiday cake. Yet these were not the things that occupied Little Nick most. He was subconsciously taken up with a completely different problem, namely, the point of view of the children. He turned his head this way and that, trying to grasp how it was possible to see a real living child in a porcelain doll, or how a piece of wood, crudely carved so that it didn't even resemble a horse, and perched, moreover, on ridiculous runners, could be considered a real horse. This unreal world of fairy tales seemed to him completely inaccessible, yet something told him it must be charming.

At night, when everyone was sleeping, the Chief would sit by the fireplace in the hall. Both he and the aged Angel allowed themselves this tranquil laying down of arms and this repose, although actually it would have been their duty to invade people's dreams. They often conversed about abstract subjects, but occasionally they talked shop. Little Nick would sit at the Chief's feet, playing with the coals. Once he inquired about what interested him most. "How can children see things that don't exist?"

"Not only children do, but grown-ups as well," retorted the Chief.

The Angel plucked a feather from his wing and poked his ear with the point.

"Well, and what is my worthy colleague's opinion?" he interjected. "Do they act thus from an overabundance or a lack of imagination?"

"I am inclined to think that it is from lack of experience. They simply do not live long enough."

The Angel smiled with forbearance.

"You see, little one," he said turning to Little Nick, "people have a lamentable tendency to break out of the circles of Good and Evil, and they seek forbidden things along seductive paths. Were they to live long enough, they might have gained a perspective which would go beyond the scope allotted to them. Since their lives are short, they waste time on queer fantasies which are too tenuous to be opposed to Evil and Good."

"My worthy colleague is quite right," said the Devil. "If humans were to break out of the circle of their imperfection, neither I nor you, my colleague, would have anything to do."

"And is Perfection perhaps similar to Truth?" asked Little Nick, recalling his father's words.

"Hush!" hissed the Angel.

"Hush!" hissed the Devil.

Their combined hissing fanned the fire in the fireplace. Little Nick cowered. The Angel pulled out a little bottle of holy water, took a swig, wiped his lips with his forefinger, and carefully stoppered the bottle again.

"Allow me to tell you," he began calmly, "that you are young and a trifle foolish (the Chief nodded his head in assent). Good upbringing is based on being able to tolerate the changes which take place on the surface of things, but nowise to change the essence of those things themselves. And intelligence consists in the realization that they will last forever."

"And when Eternity," blurted out Little Nick, without finishing, however, since at this point the sharp ringing of the telephone cut through the nocturnal quiet like a knife.

The imp shuddered through his entire body and, at the same time, had to admire the results of the experience of those who had been looking upon the world for untold ages: not a muscle twitched in their stony faces, just as if sudden and unexpected things belonged to the order of the commonplace and the expected. The telephone kept ringing. From the bedroom ran the young manufacturer, clad in pajamas. He seized the phone convulsively, shielding it with his left hand and speaking in a muted whisper:

"But darling . . . whatever entered your head? . . . at night yet! Good heavens! Don't get hysterical. . . . Yes, I'm leaving because. . . . No, I couldn't let you know because. . . . But nothing will be changed. Calm yourself. . . ."

"Alfred! Who's that calling?" the wife's voice could be heard from the bedroom.

"Tell the truth," said the Angel, but without conviction.

The Devil shrugged his shoulders.

"Would my esteemed colleague desire a scene? Now, at night, when everything is going so peacefully?"

And, turning to the manufacturer: "Tell her it's from the plant."

"Alfred!"

"It's from the plant, dear, sleep! The engineer just let me know about a localized fire in the dried fruits. Nothing serious."

And in a whisper into the phone:

"Listen."

There was a slam, and the manufacturer, shuffling in his bedslippers, crossed the hall.

Even before breakfast he left for the plant, excusing himself with the same lie. Nonetheless, the dreadful scene took place right after breakfast. The Wench ran in, apparently without any makeup on, but so stirred up and so rosy from the morning chill that, to Little Nick, she seemed even more beautiful than before. Actually he understood nothing of her complicated pretensions, nor, in general, anything about the entire involved affair. The children were immediately packed off to their rooms, and since he did not go along with them to tempt them to evil, not one of them looked through the keyhole. In the parlor the exchange of views took place ever more briskly. The last thing the Wench had just shrieked was:

"For two years he has been my lover! That is, if you really care to know!"

"He was making a fool of you!" the wife shouted, "He used to tell me all about it afterwards."

The Wench slapped the lady of the house so hard that there was an echo. The Devil grimaced with heartfelt disapproval. At this point the Angel walked up to her and whispered:

"Leave, and don't ever come back!"

Little Nick glanced at the Chief. The latter feigned not to have heard the preceding words and, approaching the mirror, for some reason or other began to feel his protruding Adam's apple, just as if he had nicked himself shaving. The serving girl was eavesdropping at the door without anyone having had to talk her into it. The Wench ran out of the house, and through the window one could see how, sobbing, bowed over, tousled, abandoned, she tottered to the waiting taxi, but could not manipulate the door handle with her trembling hand.

Suddenly, and without any apparent connection with these events, Little Nick almost literally felt the breath of Eternity. It will never end! He turned away, glanced at the wife sobbing in a corner of the divan, at the handkerchief quivering in her hand. "Yes! Yes! So Eternity will never end," he thought with bitterness.

The next day the married couple, after a long night spent together, entered the dining-room smiling, reconciled, rejuvenated somehow. The Devil leaned over the manufacturer and, with an officious gesture, said:

"Do you remember what thighs the other one had?"

From the other side, the Angel, stifling a yawn, whispered:

"Now tell me, isn't it more pleasant and easier on the soul to get rid of one's troubles?"

And the manufacturer smiled into his coffee, which he kept stirring needlessly, and finally lifted his beaming glance to his wife.

"Ah, Eternity! Eternity!" Little Nick went quietly to the other room where the children were playing. He gazed at them, picked his nose, and was suddenly overwhelmed by such a feeling of boredom and by such an urge to break out of the closed circle, that he stepped into the small mirror in the nursery and stood in the street.

It was spring. April. The sun was shining.

Little Nick thought: "To break away, break out of this circle. For a year, for three years. To live in the world of illusion." He would become visible, he decided, materialize, enter another point of view. He ran to a large department store, and not as became a self-respecting devil, but like an ordinary, human sneak thief, he lifted a little brown-checkered suit, as well as a green tie. He returned so happy, so happy!

Nothing happened at first. Only the little mirror in the nursery broke without any apparent cause. The children were awed.

"Well," cried Little Nick, "let's play! I'm just like you." And he sat down on the rocking horse. "Why doesn't it rock? Peter, give me a push."

Peter was already stretching out his hand, when the Angel suddenly seized him.

"What are you doing? That is a little imp!"

"It's not true," shouted Little Nick. "It's not true! I can see just as well as you!"

"An imp, an imp," the Angel muttered nervously. Little Nick had never seen him in such discomposure. "Shoo! Scat!" he said. "Take off! Look children, it's a little devil. Even the horse won't rock under him. Don't play with him!"

"I want to break out of this circle," cried Little Nick, but the children did not understand what his problem was.

So he climbed off the horse, and the children retreated before him. He leaned over to see if perchance a toy block hadn't fallen under the runners and prevented the horse from rocking, but suddenly he almost died of fright. The runners of the horse were held immobile by the Chief's hoof! The expression on the face of the Devil, who usually could not be made to lose his equanimity, was terrifying. "Begone!" he hissed.

"Scat!" repeated the Angel.

The hair on Little Nick's head stood up stiffer than his horns once used to. He backed away unconsciously, white as a sheet, followed by the uncomprehending glances of the children; and through their eyes Little Nick was being stalked by the Devil and the Angel. He kept backing away from them, and seeing no other means of escape, jumped, as of yore, into the fireplace. For the first time he felt the hell of fire, shrieked terribly and disappeared.

At home his mother lashed him with her tail, while his

father, grimacing, leafed through the latest issue of the
Diabolical Courier.

III

The clerk at the department store where a little child's
suit in brown checks, as well as a green tie, had disappeared, was fired. He had wanted to buy just such an outfit for his little boy's approaching birthday, and this tormented him more than the loss of his job. In despair he
went to a bar for some whisky. When he had drunk
through his money, he drank on for some time on credit.

It was spring. April. Rain was falling.

He emerged drunk, just as the street lamps were being
lighted. He walked along the boulevard near the river,
then he crossed a bridge and stopped still. In the water
he saw reflections of the lamps. Nothing but lamps. For
some reason this simple fact, without any logical connection with any other facts, prompted his decision. He
jumped over the parapet (his watch chain got caught on
some sort of hook), heard a faint tinkle, and slid under
the water.

His old hat, too greasy to sink at once, floated along
the surface of the river. For committing suicide the clerk
naturally went to Hell.

This was the first soul captured by Little Nick in his
professional life.

JERZY ZAWIEYSKI (1902–   ) is at present vice president of the Association of Polish Writers, deputy to the Polish Sejm, member of the Council of State and president of the Club of Catholic Intelligentsia. He is known chiefly as a playwright, but he has also written novels and essays as well as short stories. The recent "thaw" in Poland enabled him to break the silence he maintained during the preceding years.

ADAM CZERNIAWSKI, the translator, was born in Poland. He received B.A. honors in English Language and Literature at London University, has published a volume of Polish verse, and articles and translations in Polish and English periodicals. He wishes to acknowledge the assistance of Miss Ann Daker in preparing this translation.

The President Calls

JERZY ZAWIEYSKI

*P*aul opened his eyes for a second as the clock was striking the hour. But he had time to notice that the wall opposite was all covered in sunshine, so the day must surely have dawned a good while ago. The birds' songs had awakened him before the clock struck, but then birds get up at dawn. The only thing which worried him was the clock which had just sounded. How many times had it struck? If it was six, then at any moment Granny would be coming into the kitchen and shouting in her high-pitched voice: "Get up, you lazybones, it's six already." Paul always used to put off the moment of getting up until Granny would get cross and threaten she would complain to Father. After all, everybody was waiting for the bread which he was supposed to fetch from the baker's.

It was like that every day. Sometimes Paul would get up straight away but only if his beloved guest came before Granny's appearance in the kitchen, that is, before six. The guest would sit on the side of the bed, holding Paul's hand, or what was best of all, would bend over

213

him and kiss his forehead or his closed eyes. This guest, Mr. Venderdyke, President Venderdyke from Venderland, was Paul's wonderful secret. His voice was like Father's and he had the very soft and delicate touch Father used to have when in the past he sometimes, but only sometimes, used to stroke Paul's face.

•

On days of misfortune and sorrow and tears when there is no one to understand and help Paul, President Venderdyke often comes before bedtime. At other times President Venderdyke comes before dawn, towards the end of dreams, that is, before Granny appears. On these occasions there is usually a large sun in the sky and the birds cry out loud.

The distinguished guest from Venderland loves Paul and that is the only reason for his coming from afar, for leaving his court and hastening to Paul so that he shall not cry in his loneliness, especially when the lights are switched off.

"You may cry," the President had once explained to Paul. "It is pleasant to cry; this is the way children fight the world and grown-ups. But when you cry there must be lips which can gather up the tears. Then crying soon stops and a smile appears even before the tears—those last few drops which someone's fingers or lips have not had time to wipe away—are dry."

Whenever President Venderdyke comes he takes Paul gently by the hand and in the kindest voice, a voice like Father's, says:

"Good morning, Paul," or:

"Good evening, Paul," (depending on the time of day).

And straight away they start talking about Paul's sorrows and about Venderland. And when Paul begins to sob for no apparent reason—and that happens whenever Paul is so overwhelmed by the President's company that only tears can express it—the President kisses Paul's eyes and thus wipes away his tears, the tears of tremendous happiness.

•

Paul's wonderful secret had recently been discovered through sheer carelessness, because of his wanting too much, or perhaps because of some uncontrollable grief. On that occasion Granny had already come into the kitchen, but Paul had still gone on crying after President Venderdyke's departure:

"Please, take me with you, Mr. President. Why are you going away? Don't you like me any more? Oh, Mr. President, my dearest!"

The same thing more or less had occurred on the following day when, moreover, Paul had mentioned President Venderdyke's name several times and had stretched his arms towards him—had stretched his arms into thin air.

Granny had told Father about it and the great investigation began at lunch time: Who was this President Venderdyke? Was it someone he dreamed about? Was it a story he had heard in the kindergarten? Paul's new mummy whom Father had married three years ago because, as he had said, he couldn't stand the real mummy any more, declared that it was not worth bothering about such things: it must have been some game about the "President" made up by the lady in the kindergarten and the whole affair was just so much stuff and nonsense.

But Granny had thought differently. She maintained that Paul was ill and ought to see a doctor.

All through that debate Paul had behaved in a way most unfavorable to himself. He had refused to answer questions, kept his head bent down and pretended he was occupied with mashing the carrot on his plate. He had then proceeded to chew it slowly in case he needed an excuse for his obstinate silence. Granny had kept insisting that something was wrong with Paul and had recommended a certain institution where they treat children for such things.

"What things?" Father had asked, looking angrily at Granny.

"But these are unhealthy fantasies," said Granny in her high-pitched, melodious voice. "These are symptoms of an illness. Paul is altogether intolerable: he is obstinate, rude and shut up in himself."

"He takes after his mother," said Father. "Not very surprising: after all, she was quite mad."

And then the worst thing of all had happened. Father had pushed away his plate, lighted a cigarette, caught Paul's chin between his two fingers and laughing in that beautiful way of his had said:

"Now tell me all about this President Venderdyke. I expect he is another rascal like yourself. You eat too much before going to bed and that is why you keep dreaming of such silly nonsense."

Paul had responded in a manner that even President Venderdyke would not have approved. He had simply thrown himself on the floor, kept hitting it with his fists and crying at the top of his voice that what Father and everybody else had said wasn't true. President Venderdyke was not a game or a fairy story or a rascal, and he,

Paul, would not allow anyone to insult the true President Venderdyke.

And to crown it all Paul had declared, amid shouts and tears, that President Venderdyke had promised to take him to Venderland. "He promised! He promised!" Paul had cried in despair.

What had happened afterwards had been a justified punishment recognized as such even by Paul when, awaiting the arrival of the President that very evening, he contemplated his bad manners at table and that scene on the floor which really had been ugly and of which he was now ashamed. He had been spanked by his Father and sent to the cramped little kitchen where he could cry to his heart's content.

A little later when his Father was on his way to the city he had looked in to see Paul and had said sternly:

"Well, you've cried enough, you cry baby. Don't you worry, I'll knock that 'President' out of your head. You see if I don't!"

This then was the way in which Paul's secret had become known and everything that followed had taken the worst possible turn because Granny's point of view had prevailed and today she was taking him to that very institution where they treat children as difficult and unbearable as Paul.

Why was there no sign of Granny yet? Why wasn't she shouting that it was time for him to get up?

The clock had probably only struck five and so Paul could still wait in his half-sleep for the arrival of President Venderdyke. But would he come? Would he come?

Beyond the open windows in the gardens surrounding the house, life had begun a long while ago. The familiar bird whose song resembled a whistle kept flying from one tree to another. Its whistle was like an arrow in flight; it ended suddenly, lasting only for a moment. Other birds had more time for their singing; they did not fly so fast. Perhaps they preferred to sit on trees and sing at length a slow and unbroken melody.

It was already big Spring—that was President Venderdyke's description of it because at first there is a small Spring, then a big one, then follows a small Summer, then a big one, and after the big Summer comes small Autumn, then big Autumn, then small Winter which grows into big Winter. Out of this big Winter comes a small Spring, and after that comes the big Spring like the one now.

"Thus everything changes," Mr. Venderdyke had said. "It's the same with seasons and with man. First man is small and then big. . . ."

"But when the big man gives birth to a small one," Paul had broken in timidly, "the big one does not go away, he is still there. My Daddy and I and my new little brother Tommy, we are here and Daddy is too."

"Paul!" President Venderdyke had marveled. "You are very clever and quick, though you are only six. It is true that men are a little different from, say, Summer or Autumn, Spring or Winter. A small man and a big man may exist side by side but only for a while, only for a while. On the other hand, you can't have both small and big Spring existing side by side."

"No, indeed, you can't, Mr. President."

"You are clever, Paul, and you are also very handsome."

"But haven't I got ears that stick out and are always dirty?"

"No, your ears are regular and well proportioned."

"And haven't I got a noodle instead of a nose and bristles instead of hair? Oh, Mr. President, they always say I am ugly!"

"You have a very straight and fine little nose. And your hair is as soft as a cat's fur or the down under a guinea-hen's wings. Have you ever seen a guinea-hen?"

"Yes, I have: in a gunsmith's window. Oh, Mr. President, so I don't look ugly, do I?"

"You look very nice, Paul: I shall kiss your little nose and ears and hair."

(Paul remembers these kisses so pleasant and so very sweet as if his own Father were kissing him. But Father only kisses Paul's new little brother Tommy.

So it is big Spring, thinks Paul. Big, that means a big sun, big trees swaying their branches and lots of birds.)

He moved uneasily in his bed wedged in between the window and the scullery, because he thought he heard someone's steps. Was it Granny already? She would rush in in a hurry, knocking against the kitchen furniture. She always dressed queerly and often looked funny. This new granny, who was the mother of his new mummy, was too young and too pretty to look like a real granny. In the morning she would come into the kitchen wearing a pink dressing gown with her hair in curling-papers. She liked to paint herself and the moment she woke Paul she would disappear in the bathroom from which she would emerge with rosy cheeks, dark lines on her eyebrows and her lips bright scarlet. She had told Paul to call her "Kitty" not Granny, and he hated it. Granny did not want to be a grandmother and at the table she complained because she had to do housework and bring up children. Once she had even said she intended to get married. After all, hadn't she a right to it? The right to love? She did not wish to be left on the shelf! She had squealed excitedly and left the table—probably to have a good cry.

Daddy had choked with the food he had in his mouth, because he wanted to laugh. And when he had swallowed, said Granny was off her head.

"But Eddie, darling," the new mummy had said adjusting her spectacles. "Why should you laugh? Everyone has the right to happiness."

"I am not stopping her," Father had replied. But he kept on laughing. Mummy collected up the plates while Granny was crying in the next room because she wanted "to have a right to love."

She and Daddy did not like each other and so Paul too disliked Granny "Kitty." Not long ago she had shut Paul in one room with Tommy and told him to look after the child because she herself was going to be busy. A friend was coming to see her and she had important things to discuss with Granny. So Paul had to remain quiet, keep an eye on Tommy and not go into her room. Granny had worn her Sunday best: a string of beads pressed against her neck and she had had a red rose pinned to the left side of her dress. Her voice had been more musical than usual, she had bustled about the house and often disappeared into the kitchen from which there drifted a smell of coffee.

Granny "Kitty's" friend, as Paul had easily discovered, had a man's voice and a man's laugh. The visit had lasted a long while; Tommy was then well awake but Paul had obeyed her strictly and not gone into her room. Granny's gay conversation with her friend who had a man's voice had left Paul with an unpleasant impression and he had not failed to say so during President Venderdyke's next visit. But the President did not share Paul's opinion. He maintained that grown-ups, and especially those grown-ups whom one calls Granny or Grandpa, have odd acquaintances and even odder ways. If Granny has another visit from the friend with a man's voice and tells him not to go into her room, he must obey. And he should then turn his attention elsewhere. For example, he could calculate how long it would take a grasshopper to traverse the main avenue in the park which could be seen from the window, and how long an ant would take over it. He ought to work that out in order to keep his mind off Granny who did not want to be a granny.

"But not all grannies are like that," Paul had wanted to tell the President, but wasn't sure whether it was polite to dispute the opinions of such a wise man.

"The other granny," he sighed now. And as usual something began to choke his throat so that he couldn't swallow. It was grief, grief at the fact that the other home, the other granny, the other mummy and the other daddy no longer existed even though Daddy was still the same. But was he really the same?

When his parents were getting divorced and were to go their separate ways they had each asked which one of them he would like to stay with. Without a word he had thrown himself into his father's arms. Barbara, two years older, had stayed with Mother.

Paul had chosen his father not knowing that he would transfer to Paul all the dislike he felt for his mother. The new mummy was neither good nor bad and the same could be said about Father by an impartial onlooker like

President Venderdyke. He did not scold or beat Paul but often enough Paul would have preferred scolding and beating if afterwards his father had pressed him to his side and said something—words of forgiveness perhaps? And also provided—this was Paul's most secret desire— that on one single occasion at least his father would take him by the hand and go with him into town and that after walking thus hand in hand for a long while they would go into a confectioner's and have ice-cream.

After all, that was the way fathers walked with their little sons—a fact easily verified in parks and streets. Father never had time to take Paul on such an expedition. Since Tommy was born he never took him on his knees, never kissed him, never cuddled him. He did not like Paul putting his hands round his neck and did not like to see Paul crying because, as he had once said at table, Paul was morbidly sensitive and a cry baby.

"What will you grow up into? What will you grow up into?" He would push Paul away with harsh words like that: "You are unbearable. You are like your mother."

Paul would admit that he probably *was* like his mother; she also cried because of Father. Father did not like being loved, or at least he did not like the kind of love Paul's mother gave him. Nor did he like Paul's love.

•

Mummy and her new husband and Barbara and a real gentle old Granny all now live in another town. Occasionally, Mummy comes over and meets Paul at her sister's, Auntie Annie's. She comes for only a short while, has always lots of things to do, plenty of calls to make and never has enough time to speak to Paul or be with him and talk about everything quietly without any hurry. For couldn't he tell Mummy about the kindergarten, about what goes on in the park when it is big Spring and perhaps even about Venderland? But Mummy does not like stories—any stories—because they bore her.

"Don't bother me," is her constant reply to Paul's requests about storytelling. Whenever she comes now she has only time to kiss him on the cheek and is already rushing off somewhere. She sometimes asks: how do you get on with Father? But she does not wait for an answer because she has an urgent phone call to make or is afraid she might be late for a meeting in a coffee house.

But Paul likes her coming because he can at least look at her, watch her restless movements, her worried face, so readily covered with tears. Mummy is so tiny, so young, that when she is walking with Barbara she might be taken for her elder sister. But there is one thing Mummy always remembers: to buy Paul sweets and some expensive present. And then she departs hastily, most often unexpectedly, in response to a telegram from her new husband.

Coming back to Father after seeing Mother is a painful experience for Paul. Father makes fun of Mummy and often says she is "an idiot." Nor does he like the presents which Paul proudly shows him and always has to criticize them.

So Paul knows that Father wants him to dislike Mummy and that Mummy expects that to her question as to whether he gets on well with Father, he will reply that he doesn't, that Father is unkind or even hateful.

Paul can't take sides though he had chosen Father and had in a way abandoned his mother. That does not mean

that he has forgotten her, that he does not love her or
that he does not miss her.

•

After one of these frustrating visits by his mother,
when on Paul's return home his father had kept pointing out with more insistence than ever Paul's likeness to
"that idiotic woman"; when he had thrown away the red
Czech crayon which Paul had got as a present so that it
had rolled off the desk on to the floor and broken; when
moreover he had pushed Paul away from him—Paul's cup
of bitterness was full.

It had been evening then and Paul had had to get ready
for bed. He seemed to remember that a big Winter had
just given birth to a small Spring. Yes, it must have gone;
undressing in the kitchen he had been crying softly, not so
much with tears, but with his whole heart. Others had
mothers with whom they could laugh and play; had fathers who walked with them along park avenues or
streets, holding hands, talking merrily to each other. Why
was it then that *his* mother was away and *his* father did
not like him because he was like her? It was then that
something Paul had heard long ago had begun to grow
into a hope that he too could have someone who would
love him, who would talk to him seriously and tenderly,
would caress and kiss him. Naturally, it would have to be
his secret carefully guarded from all the world. He would
not be alone any more. He would not be alone!

Thus had been born the beloved distinguished guest:
President Venderdyke from Venderland, called forth by
desperation and the desire of the heart.

It had not surprised Paul that the President had his
father's voice and that the caresses of his hands, the

kisses, seemed to come from the most beloved one who had rejected him.

President Venderdyke was the President of all children who were deprived of love. It was exactly in this way that the President had explained to Paul that he was the President of those children who cried not knowing why, whose mothers had new husbands, whose fathers had new wives, while the children themselves had been put aside because they reminded their fathers of disliked mothers and their mothers of bad fathers.

"The country of Venderland," the President had said on that occasion, "is the land of sad children who find there what they do not have at home. It is the country of love and its name means: Everything is Good and Gay."

Again Paul moved uneasily in his little bed because he thought he heard Granny "Kitty" who would appear at any moment wearing a pink dressing gown and her golden hair twisted in curling papers. But no, there was no one walking about, no one came into the kitchen. Father and the new mummy slept in one room and Tommy slept with Granny in the other. For a moment Paul tried to think about what he was in for today, about that doctor he was to see with Granny, but he fell sound asleep.

Some moments later he heard the flight of a bird below the window. The bird gave a short sharp cry and then he felt the familiar, caressing touch on his hands.

"Good morning, Paul," said President Venderdyke.

"Good morning, Mr. President." He answered politely without opening his eyes because the best way, the only way, of seeing Mr. Venderdyke is with one's eyes shut.

"Do you know," Paul was saying, "today Granny is taking me to see a doctor who is going to knock you out of my head, Mr. President."

"Don't be afraid of anything, Paul. Grown-ups are often wrong and make false calculations. They want to knock out things which cannot be knocked out and they themselves have plenty of things in their heads which ought to be knocked out. Grown-ups are very odd and to us inhabitants of Venderland, of whom you are also one, they are not always understandable. That 'I will knock it out of your head,' is a very ridiculous grown-ups game."

"But Mr. President, I am afraid of grown-ups," sighed Paul, "I am afraid. I am afraid of that doctor I am to see with Granny 'Kitty.'"

"Don't be afraid, my dear," the President soothed him, "I shall be with you."

"Oh, good! I won't allow them to knock you out of my head, I won't, I won't!"

"Gently, little fellow, gently. . . . If you like I will tell you about Venderland. Listen: big Spring brings forth big events. Little nightingales and little cuckoos have by now been fledged because it is the time of birth among birds. And among little animals too: deer, hares and beautiful gray-blue foxes all have their young. It is the same with big animals: there are tiny lion cubs, rhinos, black bears and white bears, giraffes, fawns, camels and elephants. One can also call big Spring the period of tenderness because everything is small and so very beautiful."

At that moment the President's voice stopped because the clock began to strike the terrible hour of six.

In the hall Paul heard, this time unmistakably, the steps of Granny "Kitty."

II

The doctor was not an ordinary doctor. And he did not see his patients in his home but in a big building which had many stories, each full of doors. Facing each staircase were halls with tables where you waited your turn. It was not the Health Insurance which Paul knew from the previous year when he had gone there with Granny to have his chest X-rayed. So this is the "institution"—he thought—not being quite sure whether he had remembered such a difficult word correctly; the institution in which, Granny "Kitty" had said, they treated children like him and where they would knock President Venderdyke out of his head.

"How will they do it?" Paul thought with curiosity. He was determined not to cry because this morning he had promised the President that he wouldn't. But neither would he say anything about those wonderful visits.

Sitting on a chair next to Granny "Kitty" he watched the numerous other children who were also waiting there. Only one girl had come with her father—the other children were accompanied by their mummies or grannies. Paul found the noisy hubbub tiring; some of the children were crying while others were restless and wanted to run around or climb windows or beat other children. Granny "Kitty" was smoking a lot of cigarettes; she had taken a book out of her handbag and pretended she was reading. She certainly was pretending because Paul noticed that for a long while she had not turned the page. So she wasn't reading and occasionally glanced at Paul and at the gentleman who had brought his little daughter.

Now and then gentlemen and ladies in white coats would emerge from various doors; they were doctors. Twice a gentleman without a coat came out of a large room. He stopped by the children, stroked their hair and kept asking: "Have you come to see me? Have you come to see me?" He took Paul by the chin too and not looking at Granny asked: "Have you come to see me?" Granny stood up and said "Yes, you, doctor."

"Just a moment," the doctor replied and disappeared in his room, but before that he picked up the book Granny had dropped when she stood up to answer his question.

"What a charming doctor," said Granny, opening the book again, "and handsome."

When a little later a girl with bandy legs and a large head came out of his room the doctor invited Granny and Paul to enter. When they were already on the threshold he bent over Paul, looked carefully into his eyes and said:

"Stay in the waiting room for another second, Sonny. First we two will have a chat," and he pointed to Granny. "All right? There are picture-books on the table. I will ask you in in a minute."

So Paul returned to his seat but he did not look at any pictures because the other children had all the books. He sat on the chair, closed his eyes and tried to think back to President Venderdyke's visit in the morning. But he couldn't concentrate because of the other children constantly being told off by their mummies and grannies. Granny "Kitty's" chat with the doctor could not have lasted long because before President Venderdyke with Father's face had time to appear under his closed eyelids the doctor was already leaning over him and gently leading him by the hand to the consulting room. Granny stayed in the waiting room on a seat near the window.

The room which they went into was large with lots of light from four windows and a view of a garden. And there were plenty of toys arranged on shelves and against the walls. The doctor's desk with papers spread over it stood in the corner of the room.

The doctor led Paul to the middle of the room, then bent down and seemed to crouch beside him so that Paul did not have to keep raising his head.

"Your name is Paul, isn't it?"

"Yes, Paul."

"Do you like it here?"

"Yes, I do," he said lowering his eyes.

"We are alone now, no one is going to disturb us. I am very glad you came to see me, Paul. I would like to talk to you, you won't mind, will you?"

Paul did not answer though the doctor spoke to him in a different way from other doctors. He didn't ask him to undress or show his tongue and he didn't knock one finger against the other on his chest. But the most pleasant thing was that the doctor did not repeat his question as to whether Paul was inclined to talk. He watched Paul with a smile and stroked him gently on the head.

"Perhaps you would like to play?" The doctor suggested. "Look, there is a rocking horse. And there is an airplane. Or perhaps you would like a ship, or a train with an engine that whistles?"

The doctor got up, went to his desk and started writing. Paul shyly climbed on to the rocking horse though he was afraid he might fall off and wasn't really in the mood for playing. But he did not wish to hurt the doctor who was so polite, almost as polite as President Venderdyke. So he rocked on the horse for a while but kept thinking when and in what way the doctor would start knocking President Venderdyke out of his head and laugh at his beloved guest in the way Father had laughed on that memorable occasion when his secret had been revealed.

"You are not interested in the rocking horse, are you, Paul? Nor in the airplane? I am not really surprised," the doctor continued, "because there are children who prefer other things to toys. Grown-ups sometimes think that a horse like that or an airplane are just the things children like most, when in fact they would rather for instance be taken out for a walk and be told about the things they see around them. Sometimes they like to do the telling to the grown-ups. Isn't it true, Paul?"

"Oh yes, Mr. Pre . . . doctor," Paul corrected himself and shut his eyes tightly because he really thought it was not the doctor but President Venderdyke who has Father's voice and Father's touch.

The doctor was again leaning over, his face against Paul's, and smiling like the President.

Paul remembered that the President had promised to be with him during the examination. So perhaps there was no need to be afraid. Perhaps he ought to speak just as if he were speaking to the President?

"Please doctor, will you tell me a story?" Paul said quickly.

"Right: first I will tell you something, then it will be your turn. I am very glad you came to see me. We have plenty of time and no one will disturb us. And if we don't have time to tell each other everything, you can come to me tomorrow or the day after, whenever you like."

"I shall, I shall certainly come," Paul agreed eagerly.

And suddenly, but probably due only to the President's prompting, Paul stretched his arms out slightly and the doctor placed them round his neck and pressed his face against Paul's: so they remained for a long while in silence. Paul could control himself no longer and though he did not really want to he began to weep softly. He swallowed the tears and pressed his eyelids together tightly so that the tears would not be seen.

Luckily, the doctor did not notice anything. He took a low stool, placed Paul on his knees, put his arms round him and began to tell a story.

It was about the doctor's flight in an airplane.

Since Paul could not say anything because of the tears, the doctor went on to tell another story. It was a wonderful story which Paul decided to repeat to Mr. Venderdyke when he visited Paul that day. The doctor spoke beautifully about a little boy whom he knew and loved. About a boy who had once found a homeless dog which was very lean and scraggy. The story about the dog and the boy was very sad but the end was happy and even funny and Paul laughed as much as the doctor did because it appeared that the dog was cleverer than the boy and could for instance pull him out of a big ditch into which he had fallen through being very absent-minded. And there were many other similar adventures. The boy and the dog loved each other very much.

"Everyone has to have someone who loves him," Paul said suddenly. The doctor gave Paul a serious look and asked *him* to tell something for a change.

•

Paul is now quite sure that President Venderdyke has

kept his promise and is quite close, is certainly present at this chat which was supposed to have been an "examination." There is no examination, only a chat or rather a game; in fact something like the President's visit. Except that when the President comes Paul does not open his eyes and only sees Mr. Venderdyke under his eyelids. While now, he can look at the doctor, put his hands round the doctor's neck and laugh with him—even cry.

The doctor looks like President Venderdyke and so he looks like Father too. He has the dark hair, the pleasant voice, the smile, the way of speaking—everything like Father's, particularly when Father holds Tommy in his arms and uses words which are full of caresses. Paul is sure that the doctor will not knock President Venderdyke out of his head and that he can entrust his secrets to him. So he settles more comfortably on the doctor's knees, puts his arms round his neck and whispers into his ear about Venderland and President Venderdyke. He tells about the President's visits, describes all the events concerned with the seasons and tells about the birth of birds and animals. He tells about children abandoned by grown-ups, about the sad children who cry until they discover the marvelous country of Venderland. In that country they find what they lack at home. Then they are not alone because in the country of Venderland everything is Good and Gay.

•

The doctor listened attentively and often interrupted with: "Yes, yes, Paul, go on, go on, what then, what else?"

Then, when he reached the end of his most intimate confessions Paul asked with sudden fear:

"Doctor, you will not knock President Venderdyke out of my head, will you?"

The doctor held Paul closely in his arms and in this way assured him that he need not fear anything of the kind. After a long pause the doctor asked Paul to tell him everything about his home, everything as far back as he could remember.

So Paul went on talking, but when he got to the scene at the table when the secret about President Venderdyke was discovered, he felt a lump in his throat and could not say anything more.

The doctor did not press him. There was a long silence and nobody came in though in the waiting room there were mummies and grannies with children getting restless. The doctor had plenty of time and it seemed that the most important thing in the world for him was Paul and his secret about President Venderdyke.

In the silence which was so wonderful because during it Paul could hug the doctor who resembled both Father and the President, he heard the words:

"Tell me, Paul, what do you want most of all in the world at this moment?"

"Most of all," Paul whispered in the doctor's ear, "I would like Daddy to take me by the hand and go with me a long, long way through the streets . . . into the city . . . and tell me about . . . and that everyone would see. . . ."

Paul was ashamed of his tears because he did not in the least want to cry, but they came of their own accord.

At the end of the visit the doctor started a game of questions:

"How many legs has a large dog and how many has a small one? What is an airplane and what is a bird? Who is a soldier?"

The doctor was pleased with the game and so he kissed

Paul and thanked him for their talk. Once more he asked Granny "Kitty" from the waiting room and told her briefly that he would like to see Paul's father. Then he accompanied both of them to the stairs leading to the first floor where Paul was to be seen by a real doctor who would ask him to show his tongue and knock one finger against the other on his chest.

III

So the doctor did not knock President Venderdyke out of Paul's head and that was why he answered with exaggerated cheerfulness the impatient questions Granny "Kitty" asked him once they found themselves outside the building, but he was careful not to reveal any details relating to anything connected with his secret.

"What else, what else?" Granny badgered him. So once again Paul described the "questions" game and repeated the stories about the dog and about the airplane.

Granny was not satisfied with the visit and she particularly resented the doctor's request to see Paul's father.

At lunch Granny "Kitty" talked all the time, which was a relief for Paul because he did not have to answer questions like: "Well, and how was it? What did the doctor say? What did you do?" Father was late for lunch and felt tired because there were conferences going on in the office all the time. He did not say "Hello" to anyone except the new mummy whom he called "Maisie," took Tommy into his arms but quickly handed him back to Mummy.

Granny told Father that the doctor wanted to see him about Paul. Father replied irritably that he did not wish to be bothered, that he wouldn't even dream of going there and that this doctor Granny "Kitty" had invented was in all probability no more than a *charlatan.* Paul did not know what *charlatan* meant but he felt that it must be something nasty. And suddenly, without realizing how it happened, he cried: "It's not true, Daddy, that doctor is a very good doctor!" As a punishment Father ordered him into the kitchen. A moment later the new mummy came in to fetch the raspberry cream and while she was making the coffee for Father, said:

"You were naughty again, Paul. You ought to tell Daddy you are sorry. Children shouldn't speak like that to grown-ups."

After lunch Paul wanted to do what his new mummy had asked him and apologize to Father, because he knew quite well that you shouldn't argue with your father. Of course that did not mean that Father was right because the doctor did not deserve to be called *charlatan.*

Paul chose a moment when Father was getting ready for his afternoon nap; he came up to him but did not know what to do or say. He wanted to take Father's hand or put his arms around his neck the way he had put them round the doctor's neck that morning.

He whispered timidly:

"Daddy. . . ."

"Go away, can't you see I want to sleep?"

And Father turned his face to the wall.

Towards evening his parents went out to the theatre and so he had still had no opportunity to apologize to Father. The moment they had gone Granny "Kitty" told him to look after Tommy because she herself had to go and see a friend of hers about something very important.

She would be back in half an hour. But she returned late when Tommy was fast asleep and Paul was so tired that he could hardly sit up by his little brother's cot.

Fighting off sleep he had been calling on President Venderdyke whom he had so many things to tell about the day's events.

Granny "Kitty" returned in a cheerful mood and was nice to Paul. She gave him a bar of chocolate and hummed a tune while setting up his camp bed in the kitchen. Paul quickly washed himself in the bathroom and asking Granny to switch off the light lay down somewhat less sleepy.

After a moment of joyful expectation Mr. President Venderdyke, the beloved visitor, appeared under his eyelids.

"Good evening, Paul," he heard the sound of that most delightful voice and at the same time he felt a touch on his hands, Father's touch.

Paul began to speak. He spoke in the same way as he had done to the doctor, his face close to the President's. When he had narrated all the day's events including Granny "Kitty's" return and her merry humming in the kitchen, he asked timidly:

"Has that doctor ever been to the country of Venderland?"

Mr. President smiled affectionately, stroked Paul's face and did not say anything but went on smiling, which meant that Paul's question was not very sensible because Paul should have known what the answer would be. Had he not recognized an inhabitant of Venderland by the way he spoke, by his tender embrace, by his caressing hands, and above all, by his wonderful stories? "Oh,

Paul," President Venderdyke seemed to say reproachfully, "the country of Venderland is very large and has no limits. Grown-ups know about its existence but they avoid it because they prefer the silly game about which we talked this morning, the game with the motto: 'I will knock that out of your head. . . .'"

"Oh, but Mr. President," Paul whispered terrified, "that game will have a bad end. What if they attack us, if they conquer us and start knocking the country of Venderland out of our heads? My dearest. . . ."

"Don't cry, sonny. They will never conquer it. Never, Paul. Don't be afraid. . . ."

"Oh, Mr. President, my dearest, I feel so sad. Father is cross with me, he is always cross with me because I remind him of Mummy. What can I do? The only thing I can do is cry."

"That is why I come to you, Paul, my precious," the President said in a serious tone, "so that you will not have to cry. Put your hands round my neck. There—everything is all right now: we are in the country of Venderland."

"Yes . . . yes . . . ," Paul whispered.

"I will tell you what happened there today. A tremendous and extraordinary thing occurred."

"What was it?"

"There was a Great Music at Twilight and a Great Song. That is, as grown-ups say: a Great Concert. Or, if you like: an Evening of Music. Since dawn preparations had been in progress for the ceremonial march to the Great Concert which was to take place in a secluded forest glade. When the sun winked a sign that the time had arrived, the ceremonial procession began. It was headed by the tiniest things: the tiniest animals and the tiniest birds led by the tiniest children. None of the birds flew because the birds' parliament had decreed that they should show their kinship with those who have no wings by going on foot. Both birds and the little animals walked at a slow pace in pairs in a prearranged order: each bird was accompanied by a little animal: a nightingale by a kitten, a cuckoo by a squirrel, a lark by a little doggie, a swallow by a little hare and a sparrow by a little fox."

"I can see them walking! It is wonderful, and funny too, Mr. President!"

"Behind these came older and bigger animals: a wolf with a lamb, a calf with a boar, an ox with a giraffe, a deer with an elephant, a hind with a goat and a pony with a camel. But I really couldn't count all the pairs," President Venderdyke laughed heartily. "In the glade, then, they had a Great Concert. First, the Wind conducted a music of forest trees, a music of streams and rivers and the quiet rustle of corn fields. Even the grass, even the flowers had their share in the concert. Everything able to move was taking part together with the trees and the waters in the rivers and streams. The gathering offered thanks to the Wind with a Great Murmur of Appreciation. Then followed performances by singers. First, the nightingales sang their love songs to which the audience listened cuddling close to each other. This caused such delight that they had to sing until their throats were sore. But the most wonderful singers, Paul, were the larks. They sang so plaintively, their notes soared so marvelously that the listeners were left speechless with wonder and rapture. They were speechless, that is, they all forgot that when the larks' song was finished they ought to have growled or squeaked, each according to his nature. So there was a great silence and this was also music. The larks dropped down from above into the corn and there they fainted exhausted from sheer happiness. Thus it continued till the beaming and smiling sun went down. Later, those who heard the Great Concert returned home in pairs still under the spell. Oh Paul, that was a wonderful Venderland festival. . . ."

"Would you go with me, Mr. President," Paul spoke through tears, "would you go with me, holding me by the hand. . . ."

The President had no time to reply because the light went on and Paul's parents came in to make themselves tea from the kettle which stood over a low flame on the gas stove. The kettle was simmering quietly as if it too had been taking part in the Great Concert which President Venderdyke had described.

Through half closed eyelids Paul saw the new mummy Maisie bending over him with a cup of tea in her hand.

"He's been crying in his sleep again," she said to Father. "What are we to do with him? Eddie darling, you ought to see that doctor about Paul."

"No, I shan't," Father said harshly. "If this is going to go on he will have to be sent to his mother or placed in a Children's Home."

"But Eddie!" the new mummy was surprised. "Ah well, just as you wish," she said after a pause. "It's your child after all."

Suddenly the light went out and they both left the kitchen. They looked in to see Tommy and bent over him smiling, full of tenderness and wonder at the fact that he had placed his hands so charmingly against his little head. They gazed for a long time, their hands now round each other's waists. Then they went out on tiptoe in order not to wake the child and Granny "Kitty" who was muttering something in her sleep.

Paul heard their steps and the clatter of plates and glasses. Then there was silence. He was now quite alone. Again and always alone.

Into the terrifying darkness of the night he stretched out his hands and called President Venderdyke to come and take him to the country of Venderland. To take him before this horrible thing that Father had spoken about could happen to him.

MAREK HŁASKO (1931–   ) is a new light in the Polish literary world. There are, somewhat unexpectedly,
traces of Hemingway and Steinbeck in what he has thus
far written. Though his stories are earthy—even bawdy—
they are protests against conditions in Poland and appeals
for the validity of basic human ideals. It is to be hoped
that his undeniable talent will develop.

WOJCIECH GNIATCZYŃSKI, one of the translators, is
a native Pole who received his B.A. at the University of
Ireland. A biographical note on ADAM CZERNIAWSKI,
the co-translator, is contained on page 212 in connection
with another story translation.

The Most Sacred Words of Our Life

They woke at dawn, clinging so tightly and closely to each other that their first reaction was surprise at having passed the night in a deep and healthy sleep which their closeness had not interrupted. The boy moved and lifted himself up on his elbow; with burning eyes he watched the girl for a moment, then said:

"If it's really you, say something out loud."

The girl laughed. She embraced his head with her naked arms and hugged him close; she was warm like bread. For a moment he listened to the hard beating of her heart, then she said very softly:

"Do you think this is a dream?"

"I don't know anything," he said, "and you don't know how many nights you had already been with me, spoken to me, laughed to me. You told me things of which I used to dream and when morning came and I woke up there was an empty space by my side."

He touched her face with his hand and said:

"Who knows?"

"Do you still think it's a dream?"

"I'm telling you: who knows?"

She looked at him through narrowed eyes. He knew she wanted to tell him something but was hesitating. In sudden fear he pressed her hand and she said:

"Well then, I'll tell you what you should do. Get up and go to the mirror."

"What for?"

"Just get up."

The boy got up. He went to the window and drew back the curtains. The day was bright and clear, the roofs glittered with dew. It was early: only the first street-cars rattled along. He watched the empty street for a while, then said:

"I'm a little scared."

She jumped out of the bed. She took him by the hand and led him to the mirror.

"Do you believe me now?" she asked. "Dreams bite the soul, my dear, but not the neck."

"Don't you regret this?"

"What?"

"The night."

"If I regretted it you wouldn't look as you do. Do you think one can love somebody like this, if one doesn't desire him?"

"Did you ever think of me before?"

"Often."

"Did you want this?"

"Certainly as much as you did."

He smiled bitterly.

"Do you know," he asked, "how much I wanted you?"

"Oh, I do: I'll have to cover up my neck as well, so that people won't see it."

He was overtaken by a terrible, sad emotion—almost regret.

"I waited for all this so long," he mumbled. "I dreamt. . . . It's almost awful to think that all of it has already happened."

He walked to the window and looked at the street again. He did not want to speak, he was afraid of words. People were beginning to come out of the houses on their way to work. He knew them all; it was a small sandy street, the sort in which even nowadays people know each other's dreams. Filled with a strange, heavy emotion of happiness in which he still couldn't believe, he kept silent. He didn't turn round till he heard her voice. She stood behind him, her face touching his back, and said:

"You smell of milk like a little puppy, how funny. And you have strange eyes. . . ." She took his face in her hands and said: "You really are a little puppy. If only it could go on like this forever. I was never so happy with any man. I never felt so good with anybody else. I swear to you: I hadn't even dreamt that I would ever be so happy."

"Did you like it?" he asked, feeling his heart leap into his mouth.

"Oh, don't ask," she said. "Now I am beginning to feel everything was only a bad dream."

"A bad one?"

"Because you're sorry only when good dreams come to an end."

"I tell you what you ought to do."

"Go to the mirror."

"Exactly."

They both laughed. The boy said:

"I must be off to work now."

"Eat your breakfast."

"I can't," he said and shook his head sadly. "You know how it is when one is late for work."

"Wait, I'll fix something for you to take along."

He began to put on his clothes. Doing this he didn't dare touch his body. He still felt her next to him: to the very tips of his hairs he was overflowing with this strange feeling which is heavier than lead, more painful than the agony of dying, sweeter than the most beautiful verse, and which one has after a night spent with someone for whom one has waited endless thousands of moments, whom one had desired for countless sleepless nights, whom one saw in every face met in the street, whom one expected at every knock at one's door; because of whom one hated the sky, the earth and people; because of whom one loved everything.

"When will you come?" the girl asked.

"Tonight. Will you wait?"

"Why ask?"

"I am still frightened."

"I'll be home first."

"Switch on the light, draw back the curtains and wait for me."

"I'll switch on the light, draw back the curtains and wait for you. And now I will tell you something: we won't say good-bye."

"Why?"

"I don't want to part with you even for a moment."

He shut the door behind him and ran downstairs like a shot. In the street he breathed in the fresh air. "Aah," he sighed. He raised his head and waved to her. Then he moved off quickly. He had rather a long way to work and since it was late he had to hurry. He stopped in front of a house and shouted:

"Joe, come on, come on!" and because like every Warsaw smart guy he pronounced words as though he had no teeth it sounded like: "Jow, come ow, come ow!"

Joe came out. He was short and sturdy, his face benevolent and wide. He was dressed like the boy: in a mechanic's black overalls; his colorful shirt unbuttoned at his hard neck.

"Hi," he said. "Let's step on it. We still got to call Malinowski and Gene. Step on it: I've been late for work twice already this month."

They walked fast. The sun was already high in the sky. The dew on trees, roofs, leaves and grass was drying up quickly. There were women walking along the street. Their hair was disheveled; they carried bottles, pots and jugs for milk. Joe said:

"Drop in at our place tonight. Fanfan is bringing a record player. There'll be a bottle too."

"Can't tonight," said the boy. "Tonight I am busy."

"Seeing Barbara?"

"None of your business."

"Oh God," said Joe dreamily, "what a lovable girl. Oh God, how I loved her! She always used to tell me: 'You smell of milk like a little kitten.'"

"You're lying, you bastard!"

"May I have such luck all my life! Look, you know I ain't one to kid you. She used to say I was like a little furry puppy. Keep your shirt on. She was a whore long before we got tricked. Oh God, how I loved her—and she dropped me."

"She couldn't have told you that!"

"No?"

"No. You want to make something of it?"

"Wait."

They stopped in front of a house. Joe called: "Malinowski, come out!"

Malinowski came out. He was a young man, lively and graceful. Needless to add, like all the boys he wore his hair à la Fanfan, the movie character, and, since he had the prettiest hair of them all, it was to him that the honorable nickname fell.

"Hi," said Fanfan.

"Fanfan," said Joe, "tell him: what did Barbara say to you when she fiddled on your flute?"

"It's late," said Fanfan. "They've told me that if I'm late again they'll let me have it. We always go to bed late, that's the trouble. Barbara is a good girl, Joe. I won't let anyone say anything against her."

Joe got impatient.

"That's not what I'm talking about," he said gasping for breath. They were walking fast and his were the shortest legs. "Am I asking you to say anything against her? I loved her more than you did, Fanfan, that's for sure. And you know why she dropped me. But then she always did speak so beautifully."

Fanfan ruffled his hair and said:

"You are my little honey bear."

"And about the puppy."

"Sure there was a puppy," said Fanfan. "She said that

I smelled like a puppy, a small puppy." He turned to the boy.

"Drop in to Joe's tonight. I'm borrowing a record player from my brother-in-law."

"I can't," said the boy softly. "I'm busy tonight."

"There goes Gene," said Fanfan and shouted: "Hey, Gene, wait a minute!"

Gene, the man walking in front of them, halted. He had the face of a drunk, his eyes were bloodshot.

"Hi," he said flipping the visor of his cap with his finger.

"Hi."

"Hi."

"Oh God Almighty," said Gene hoarsely, "am I burning. If I could only buy some beer some place."

"It's late already. We'll have to ride on the knockers as it is. It's crowded like hell at this time," said Fanfan. Gene looked at the boy with his bloodshot eyes and said sympathetically: "What's eating you, Sweetie-pie? Romantic variations on a theme, right?"

"Lay off," the boy said.

"He's become very queer lately," Gene said with an expression of pain on his face. He was tortured by a gloomy hangover feeling. He said:

"You must lay a pretty girl. It'll pass."

"Sure thing," said Fanfan and spat.

"He's already got a pretty girl," said Joe. "You know his doll, don't you, Gene?"

"Which one? Christ, am I thirsty."

"That one round the corner."

"Barbara?"

"Sure."

"You bet," said Gene and his twisted face brightened up for a moment. "You'll be lucky in life if you get what I lost on her. She's the prettiest doll down here in Marymont. Wait a minute. What was it she used to say? Jesus, I'll die of thirst."

"Milk, Gene. Best thing for a hangover," said Fanfan.

"Goddam," croaked Gene and twisted his face again as though he had tasted vinegar. "That's just it: milk. They always say something. When I was your age I was just beginning to lay them. At that time every girl would still say you were the second one. You bet. And the first one was always a partisan who got killed—in a forest of course. And a year later, when they were through with forests, a girl would tell you this partisan of hers was either in a cage or the Security blew his brains out. Sure thing. 'When I was young I met a soldier who looked into death's eyes every day and I wanted to give him some happiness because something told me he would die . . .' and so on. You bet. Lovely stories. I've heard lots of them in my time. Every girl then had her Lieutenant Joe in the Home Army. Now this one hadn't 'cause she was too young. But she too used sweet words on me and I laid her and wept: I'm a lush and I've a soft heart. Yakitty yak."

"That's not the point," said the boy with despair. "That's not the point at all. But, Gene, did she tell you she had never been so happy with any man as she was with you? Did she?"

"She did," said Gene.

"She did," said Fanfan.

"She did," said Joe.

"Did she tell you she never even dreamt of being so happy with a man?"

"She did."

"She did."

"She did."

"Did she say good-bye when you were leaving for work in the morning?"

"No," said Fanfan. "We never said good-bye."

"No," said Joe and his ugly face became sad.

"No," said Gene. "Wait a minute, I'll holler for my brother-in-law. Dammit, it's late."

They stopped in front of a house. It was an old, repulsive, shabby house; one of those houses in front of which it is enough to stop and take only one look to see a heap of miserable existence; just one look and you hope that the door of this house will forever be closed to you. There are still many, many such houses in the sandy, crooked streets of the suburb known as Marymont.

"Well, I'll be off," said the boy. "There's some business I've got to settle. I won't wait for your brother-in-law. See ya tonight."

"But you said you weren't coming," said Joe. "You were going to be busy tonight."

"I'll come," said the boy. "I'll settle it now. So they'll kick me out of the job—who cares?"

"Anything important?"

"What's it to you? Fanfan, you just show up with that record player. See ya," he said and went back in the direction he had just come.

"See ya," said Fanfan.

"See ya," said Joe.

"See ya," said Gene and again twisted his face terribly.

Then he said, shaking his head: "What the hell's the matter? He was such a nice kid. . . . Help him you guys. He should find a girl who will fall in love with him, who'll tell him something swell, something sacred. I swear to God Almighty that all he needs is just a girl like that. Help him: what the hell, are you his pals or not?"

Manuscript edited by Francis T. Majeske

Designed by Richard Kinney
Set in Linotype Caledonia
Engravings by Universal Engraving Co.
Printed on Warren's Olde Style Antique Wove
and bound in Bancroft Arrestox and Elephant Hide paper
by American Book-Stratford Press, Inc., New York